Meal by Meal

Reduce Bodyfat with Low Carb and Other Diet Recipes

Dixie Henry and Betty Crawford

Table of Contents

Introduction

Body fat and being overweight is a big deal for so many people. Diets and fads come and go. People will sing praises of them only to turn around and gain every ounce they lost back just as fast as they lost it. If you go on just "one" kind of diet, it may not work. Few people can stick with just one diet. Perhaps you are the type of person who needs to diet but gets bored or tired of the same foods. It would be nice to pick and choose from a variety of diets which all have one thing in common, they aid in weight loss. That's what this book is, a compilation of several different diet plans, the best of the best. It gives you a big choice in variety so you won't become dissatisfied with the plan.

Dieting Success

The true success of a diet plan lies in whether or not you accomplish your goals of weight loss and whether or not you maintain that weight loss. So many people will fail on diets because they do not make it a lifestyle change. Sure, you can go on a particular diet and lose all the weight you want to lose. The failure comes in when once you've lost the weight you go right back to your old eating habits. You will find the weight just piles right back on your body. You must think of your diet as a lifestyle change. You must realize what put the body fat on you in the first place, your poor eating habits. This change must be permanent. When you go on this new diet, make it a lifestyle change and make it permanent.

If you want to start the diet right you need to take a couple of weeks to prepare for it. This gives you time to break the junk food addiction. This addiction is a strong one and is one of the main reasons why so many fail at their diets. If you take the time to break it you will have a better chance to succeed with the diet changes and burn off the body fat.

It may help to know junk food addiction is as strong an addiction as to smoking. While you can quit smoking just by stopping suddenly, the withdrawal symptoms are terrible and the cravings are too intense. It is the same way with junk food addiction. If you take the time to wean slowly, you will be able to handle any withdrawals because they will not be as severe, if you have withdrawals at all. Food addiction withdrawals include headache, mood swings, and intense cravings.

It takes about three weeks to break a bad habit such as a junk food addiction. Take a week and keep a food journal to give you an accurate picture of your eating habits. Record what you eat, how much you eat, and your mood at the time. This will tell you how much junk food you are eating. It will also tell you if you are a nervous eater, depressed eater, or even a bored eater. Ideally, we should only eat when we are hungry, but so many people will eat to help with their emotions or boredom. This adds to the overweight issues.

Once you determine how much junk food you eat you will see how addicted you are. There are two good ways to wean from junk food. You can choose the way in which you feel most comfortable.

The first way is to cut back on one instance of eating junk food every three to five days. Every three to five days cut back another instance by eliminating the junk food and replacing it with a healthy snack. By the time three weeks roll around you will have busted the junk food addiction.

The second way is to cut down to eating junk food just once a day for a week. Week 2, eat junk food once every other day. Week 3, eat junk food once every three days. Then, if you are still addicted stick with eating junk food, just one times a week. You can adjust this as you need to.

Other alternative ways to break the junk food habit is to eat junk food three times a day for five days. Then eat junk food twice a day for five days, and then eat it just once a day for five days. After that go a week by skipping a day between and then go a week skipping two days, then three, and end up with eating it just once a week. By that time, you should be over the junk food addiction. You should have overcome it easily without the painful withdrawal symptoms.

Let's Get Physical

Physical activity is a great way to help trim the body fat and it works wonderfully with dieting. Exercise does not mean you have to join a gym and work out every day. For optimum benefit with exercise, you should commit to working out every other day for a minimum of thirty minutes. You can walk, swim, ride bikes, jog, and run, do aerobics, dance, or join a gym if you wish. As long as you work out enough to break a sweat, you are doing well. The body needs physical activity. We can blame sedentary lifestyles for most of the weight issues today coupled with the junk food addiction. Working out also helps to boost the metabolism so you will have more energy. It helps to strengthen the immune system too.

Disclaimer

Always seek the advice and counsel of your health care provider before starting any new diet or exercise routine. What you read here is for informational purposes only. The recipes are healthy and nutritious and most people can consume them with no problem. You will see good results if you get on the diet and stick with the diet.

Section 1: Dieting Cookbook

Is losing weight easy? Well, the answer to that question depends a lot on how you define the word "easy."

Many do want to take the easy way out and this is rarely a good idea.

If you are looking for a diet that can help you shed 15lbs in a month, there are no easy answers. Then again, that statement can be amended slightly. You can lose quite a lot of weight in a month if you take advantage of fad diets that entail starving yourself via calorie restriction. No one will deny those diets will help you lose weight. Granted, the weight you lose will be mostly water and muscle. Anyone looking to target fat will find these diets do not deliver on expectations.

There also is that nasty little thing about crash diets leading to binge eating. Of course, once you go on an over the top binge, you will find yourself gaining all that weight you tried to lose in the first place, plus more on top of it.

No, none of these dietary strategies is a good one and they do not contribute one iota to losing weight for the long term and keeping it off. If long term weight loss is your real goal, you will want to eat healthier. That means you want to eat good food that is low in calories and fat.

Healthy recipes are where it's at! This is the true path to smart and, dare it be said, easy weight loss.

At this point, you are probably mentioning the well-worn cliché that doing so is a lot easier said than done. There are not exactly many healthy food choices available to those wishing to drop weight. Super markets are loaded with processed foods that do not actually do a body good.

There is certainly quite a bit of truth to that statement. No honest person would ever note that processed, sugary and fatty foods do not crowd supermarket store shelves. Sure, those items are there and they are joined by a lot of healthy selections. All you have to do is take these selections and make your own diet healthy and conscious food choices.

NO, it is not all that difficult to cook breakfasts, lunches and dinners that are good for you and can help you lose weight. Even those that are not well versed in the art of gourmet cooking can make scores of amazing food selections. Tons of these recipes are easy to prepare and, generally, do not take very long to cook. Some of these recipes do not even need to be cooked!

Whether you are interested in the traditional low fat diet or the popular low carb diet, there are recipes here for you. Do you want breakfasts or even desserts to help you lose weight? You have a number of them to choose from. Are you considering flirting with muscle building, raw food or the Paleo diet, this book offers a small glimpse into a few of those recipes.

So, if you want to lose weight and never get bored eating or cooking in the kitchen, you can let your journey to a healthier (and funner) life begin...

Chapter One

Low Fat Recipes: The Basic Weight Loss Recipes

Without a doubt, low fat diet recipes are among the most common and popular ones for those wishing to lose weight. This should not come as too much of a surprise. Fat is loaded with calories and if you eat a high fat diet, you are likely to pack on a lot of unwanted and unnecessary weight. Food selections that are low in fat generally are safe bets for those wishing to shed pounds.

(And then there is the little matter of a low fat diet being good for the heart)

There are only three things food can be comprised of: fat, carbohydrates and protein. The lower the fat amount, the higher the protein and the carbohydrates will be. Now, you do not want those carbs to be bad ones. Bad would be defined as carbs made of refined sugar. You will want natural carbs and those that are low in overall calories. Food selections such as these will help you maintain the overall calorie levels required to help you lose the weight.

Low fat foods are generally light and, quite honestly, often easy to prepare. Even if you are somewhat new to cooking, you will find quite a few of these recipes to be easy to make.

They are also commonly very healthy for you and that is a good thing when you are concerned about weight loss. Losing weight is not just about how you look. It is also about your overall health and wellbeing.

To start you on your journey to better and healthier living, here are a few low fat recipes to give a try:

Baked Salmon

One Salmon Filet (14oz)
Salt & Pepper

Turn the oven on and preheat it to about 400 degrees, Cut a 14-ounce salmon fillet into four equal size pieces.

Sprinkle the salmon fillets with a little bit of salt and pepper for seasoning and taste.

Put the salmon on a baking sheet and place it in the oven. Allow the salmon to cook for up to 15 minutes or until fully done.

Baked Pork (or lamb) Tenderloin

Ingredients:

Pork (or lamb) Tenderloin
Garlic powder, ground cumin, dried thyme, ground coriander, minced garlic and dried oregano
Olive oil

An oven will need to be preheated to 450 degrees Fahrenheit.

Take a small bowl and mix in the various different dry ingredients, which will include one teaspoon each of garlic powder, ground cumin, dried thyme, ground coriander, and dried oregano. This mix is to be stirred evenly until it turns into a single seasoning for the pork.

On a cutting board, place one and a half pounds of pork tenderloin. Rub in the new seasoning mixture you have made and be sure to run it in on the top and the bottom of the pork. Make sure the seasoning is rubbed in evenly and no portions of the pork should be missed. You might have to rub the seasoning somewhat hard into the surface so the seasoning does not fall off the pork.

Heat a tablespoon of olive oil on a skillet on the stove.

The heat should be about medium level. Sauté one teaspoon of minced garlic in the oil. Stir it up for about a minute.

Place the pork tenderloin in the skillet and cook it for ten minutes. Be sure both sides are cooked. You will want to turn the pork over to ensure this is the case. (It might be best to turn it over with large tongs as it could slip off a fork)

Remove the pork from the skillet and put it in a roasting pan. The pan is to go into the oven where it will bake for upwards of 20 minutes or until done.

Grilled Marinated Chicken

Ingredients:

Two Chicken Breasts
Dijon mustard
Lemon juice
Worcestershire sauce
Black pepper
Dried tarragon

Take a large plastic bag with a zip seal and pour in one-quarter cup of Dijon mustard along with two tablespoons of lemon juice, one and a half tablespoon of Worcestershire sauce, a quarter teaspoon of black pepper, and a half a teaspoon of dried tarragon.

Take two chicken breasts and cut them in half. This will leave you with four boneless breast halves that may weigh about five ounces each.

The chicken halves are then to be cut in the bag and allowed to marinate. Among the best ways to do this would be to place the bag in the refrigerator and leave it there for several hours. This will allow the marinate juice to fully soak into the chicken.

Remove the chicken from the bag. Allow the excess marinade to drain off from it.

The chicken can them be placed on a grill (medium heat) for a little over ten minutes or until done.

(Mostly) Homemade Low Fat Vegetable Lasagna

Ingredients:

Organic lasagna noodles
Carrots, julienned green pepper, red pepper, yellow squash, zucchini, broccoli florets, onion, and celery
Vegetable oil
Garlic cloves
Tomato sauce
Mozzarella cheese

Boil one dozen organic lasagna noodles in water. Once they are suitably softened, take them out of the pot and allow them to completely and fully drain.

Preheat an oven at around 350 degrees.

Make the Vegetable Mix:

Take two medium sized carrots and cut them into very long and thin strips. (This type of cutting is called julienned cutting)

Make a half a cup of julienned green pepper and a half a cup of red pepper (sweet)

Cut both a yellow squash and a zucchini into one-third of an inch slices.

Slice a single onion.

Slice one half of a cup of celery.

Measure out about one cup of broccoli florets.

Place a skillet on the stove and lightly heat vegetable oil on it. Pour in all the vegetables and stir-fry them while adding a small pinch of salt. Allow the vegetables to become browned. Once they are crispy, you can then out two minced cloves of garlic and stir the mix up for about another minute.

Make the Lasagna:

Take a baking dish and spray it with a non-sticking solution. Add about two-thirds of a cup of organic spaghetti marinara or vegetable sauce. Place a half dozen of the noodles over the sauce. Put two-thirds of the vegetable mix over the noodles. Pour on top of the vegetables the rest of your chosen spaghetti sauce. Top with four full cups of low fat mozzarella cheese. The remaining half dozen noodles over the sauce, veggies and cheese. Add the remaining vegetables and cheese to the lasagna.

Cover the pot and put it in the oven for an hour or until fully done.

Baked Tilapia

Ingredients:

Five tilapia fillets
Black pepper
Lime

An oven should be preheated to about 350 degrees Fahrenheit,
Spray an oven pan with nonstick spray that has a buttery taste.

Preheat oven to 375 degrees F. Coat a large cast iron pan with a nonstick butter spray.

Take about five tilapia fillets and rinse them in the sink. Afterwards, place them on a plate and allow the fish to dry.

Season the fish with salt and a little bit of black pepper.

Take a lime and grate it for zest. Add the zest to the fillets and squeeze a little lime juice on the fish.

The fish should then go in the pan.

Once in the pan, a small amount of butter can be cut and placed on top of the fillets.

The pan then goes into the oven where it should cook for about ten full minutes.

Lean Ground Beef Wrap Sandwich

Ingredients:

Lean ground beef
Lettuce
Tomato
Onion
Salt & pepper
Worcestershire Sauce

Take a half a pound of lean ground beef and mash it out in a patty.

Place the patty in a George Foreman or similar grill and allow it to cook the meat while draining the fat. Of course, the meat can be place on a regular grill as well.

Take a head of lettuce and tear off three or four huge leaves.

Slice three or four piece from a tomato and slice about one-quarter of a fresh onion.

When the beef is done, place it in the lettuce leaves. Add salt, pepper, and two teaspoons of Worcestershire sauce.

Add the tomatoes and onions and wrap the lettuce around the beef.

Green Peppers Stuffed with Turkey

Ingredients:

Ground turkey
Green Peppers
Brown rice
Garlic clove
Diced onion
Can of tomato soup

Your oven should be preheated to about 350 degrees.

Take two medium green peppers and cut off their tops. Take out the innards and seeds.

Boil a pot of water and put the green peppers in the water for a little over four minutes. Lower the heat to medium once the peppers are put in the pot. After four or five minutes, take out the peppers and put them on a plate with a paper towel. This will allow the peppers to drain.

Cook one cup of brown rice on a pot on the stove.

Heat a frying pan on the stove and sauté a minced garlic clove and a diced onion. After three minutes or so, add a half a pound of ground turkey to the pan and cook and flip until brown.

On the turkey, season with one-quarter teaspoon of red pepper flake, one-half a teaspoon of both poultry seasoning and Italian seasoning. Pour one tablespoon of Worcestershire sauce on the turkey.

Pour a full can or organic tomato soup and the cup of cooked brown rice on the ground turkey. Allow the turkey, rice and soup to cook for three minutes. Set aside to cool slightly.

Prepare a baking dish with nonstick cooking spray.

Stuff the green peppers with the turkey and rice mix. Put the pepper tops back on the peppers and put them in the oven for 25 or so minutes. Take them out, take off the tops and add about one-quarter of a cup of shredded Cheddar cheese to the top of the peppers and put back in the oven until melted.

Chicken Cacciatore in a Slow Cooker

Ingredients:

Chicken thighs
Can crushed tomatoes
Mushrooms
Chopped onions
Green bell pepper
Organic chicken broth
Tomato paste
Oregano
Salt
Dried Basil

Take one pound of chicken thighs. De-bone the chicken and remove the skin. Take the chicken meat and choice it up into somewhat small pieces. Put this aside on a plate and now go to work on the other ingredients to mix in with the chicken.

In a large bowl, pour in a large can of crushed tomatoes along with one cup of sliced mushrooms, one and cup of chopped onions. Cut a green bell pepper into strips and put those strips into the bowl with the other ingredients. Add one-quarter of a cup of organic chicken broth to the bowl and a tablespoon of tomato paste. Mix the contents of the bowl up a little bit.

Also to be added to the bowl are three-quarters of a teaspoon of dried oregano and salt. A half a teaspoon of dried basil and a quarter teaspoon of red pepper flakes and ground black pepper. Stir up all these contents in the bowl.

The chicken and the mix are to be placed in a slow cooker where it will be stirred. Let it cook on high for four hours or until done. When you serve it, you may serve it alone or on pasta.

Homemade Beef Stew

Ingredients:

Lean cubed stewing beef
Organic tomato sauce
Water
Worcestershire sauce
Black pepper, thyme and marjoram
Beef bouillon
Potatoes (2), zucchini, yellow onions, mushrooms, celery, and carrots

Put a large and deep skillet on the stove and heat up at medium level. A full pound of lean cubed stewing beef is to be placed in the skillet where it can cook until browned. Three minutes might be enough to fully brown it.

Pour into the skillet a can or organic tomato sauce along with two full cups of water and a tablespoon of Worcestershire Sauce. Stir. Now, some herbs can be added to the skillet. These herbs come in the form of one-quarter teaspoon of ground up black pepper and one teaspoon each of thyme and marjoram. One and one-half teaspoon of beef bouillon should be put in the skillet. All of this is to be stirred so it mixed together well. Let the contents come to a boil. As soon as it is boiling, lower the heat and allow it to simmer for up to a full hour.

Scrub, peel and cube two potatoes; peel and slice two carrots; cut a zucchini in half and cut it into slices; and dice up a medium yellow onions. Mix all this into the simmering skillet with a cup of sliced mushrooms and a slice celery stalk. Let the stew simmer for another half an hour. Afterwards, include one cup of peas and let it simmer for another ten minutes.

Chapter Two

Low Carbohydrate Recipes: Somewhat Misunderstood but Very Helpful for Weight Loss

There is quite a bit of controversy surrounding low carbohydrate diets. Many nutritionists have made very negative statements about this type of diet. At the core of the criticism would be the notion this diet is unhealthy and lacking in nutrients. Others have referred to it as little more than a mere crash diet dressed up under the banner of losing weight in a simple manner.

Here is the truth: many low carb diets do embody all of these negative traits. Far too often, those wishing to lose weight via cutting carbs will cut them immensely and eat truly unhealthy and limited choices. They might eat a lot of cheese, hamburgers without the buns, bacon and eggs, and the like. Is this a diet? In the sense, you will lose weight due to the lack of insulin spiking carbs, but you probably will be on the path towards binging on carbs in the future.

Such an approach is NOT a diet in the sense of eating a

series of meals that are quite well balanced while, at the same time, maintaining a limit on the carbohydrates you are eating. Really, it is the overindulgence of carbohydrates or eating carbs too late at night is what contributes to weight gain.

If eating too many carbs has contributed to your gaining of excess weight, then you will have to take steps to cut them back. Fair enough, right? Do you do this by eating a wacky meat only diet for your meals? No, you definitely do not have to take this route. There are actually quite a number of quality low carb meals you can eat. The following are some excellent choices for breakfast, lunch, dinner and dessert for the low carb eater.

Egg Frittata

Ingredients:

Eggs
Meats if wanted
Mixed vegetables
Olive Oil
Salt & pepper
Cheese

An Egg Frittata is good for both breakfast and, with a nice salad, is great for lunch. It is also easy to make.

You take a skillet and add a small amount of oil on the skillet and lightly heat it on the top oven rack.

Raw meats can be added to the skillet. Meat does not come with any carbs so this is fine. The inclusion of raw vegetables can be put in the skillet and, even though veggies have some carbs, the amount of them is low. Cooked meats and vegetables can be put in the skillet as well.

Eggs will need to be whipped to create the frittata. The more eggs you use, the thicker the frittata will be. The fewer eggs, the thinner it will be. While whipped eggs will then have a salt and pepper added to the mix. Three tablespoons of cream, milk, water, or half and half to the mix.

If wished, add half the serving cheese you want in the Frittata to the eggs at this time.

Cook the eggs at a moderate level of heat on top of the stove for roughly two minutes. Stir the eggs until they are half cooked. Once the underside of the eggs is cooked for another minute, place the skillet in the broiler after sprinkling the remainder of the cheese on top of it.

Let it cook in the broiler for about two minutes or until the top is brown.

Let it cool and when it has cooled, cut it in wedges and serve.

Tuscan Chicken with Tomato-Basil Relish

Ingredients:

Chicken breasts
Sweet pimientos
Plum tomatoes
Salt & pepper
Olive oil
Relish

Mix a selection of one-quarter cup of sweet pimientos, one-half cup of diced plum tomatoes, and one-quarter cup of basil in bowl with a little vinegar. Put a little salt and pepper to the mix and set the bowl on the side.

Take three-quarters of a pound of white, boneless chicken breasts and flatten it out with a mallet. Place the chicken on a skillet at medium/high heat. Add a little olive oil to the skillet.

Once the skillet is heated, you put the chicken on it and sauté each side for about three minutes. Add salt and pepper to the chicken.

Once done, you can cut the chicken into the appropriate servings and then spoon the homemade relish on top of it.

Buffalo Chicken Salad

Ingredients:

Chicken breasts
Hot Sauce
Olive oil

Preheat your broiler. Take two boneless, 8-ounce chicken breast halves with no bones or skin and pound them with a mallet so the chicken ends up being even in thickness. Cut the chicken into strips about a half an inch thick.

In a bowl, pour in about two tablespoons of hot sauce along with two teaspoons of olive oil. Place the chicken strips in this mix and toss the contents until the chicken is covered with oil and sauce.

Place the chicken on a baking sheet and cook it for a little over five minutes. Turn it once.

Cut up about eight cups of the heart of Romaine lettuce and mix it in a bowl with four chopped celery stalks, two fully grated carrots, and sliced green sections of scallions. Toss these contents with one-half a cup of Blue Cheese dressing.

Combine the chicken with the salad and you are done.

Low Carb Key Lime Pie

Ingredients:

Lime gelatin
Heavy cream
Cream cheese
Sweetener
Ground pecans
Coconut extract
Butter
Ground nuts

Take a medium sized bowl and mix it with one full cup of ground pecans. Include a half-teaspoon of coconut extract, two small packets of sweetener, and three tablespoons of melted butter.

Take this mix and press it firmly into a pie plate. Place the plate in the refrigerator until the mix hardens.

Acquire a small bowl. Whip a half a cup of heavy cream in the bowl along with two packets of sweetener. Set the mix on the side.

Take a large bowl and mix 6 ounces of sugar free lime gelatin along with one-third cup of boiling water until all the gelatin has been dissolved. Then you stir in one-third cup of cold water. Cut up 16 ounces of cream cheese into cubes and put it into the bowl. Beat it with an electric mixer. Stir in about a half a teaspoon of coconut extract and beat the mixture again at very high speed. Whipped cream one-half a cup) then has to be carefully folded into the mix.

Spread the mix around the pie pan. Sprinkle about two tablespoons of ground nuts on top and then place in a refrigerator to help the gelatin set.

Chapter Three

Muscle Building Recipes to Boost the Metabolism

Far too often, people become concerned with how to lose weight by cutting down on their calories. While cutting calories will certainly keep weight down, there are other issues you do have to be wary of. Namely, a speeded up metabolism will play a major role in burning off fat. While there are quite a number of ways you can speed up your metabolism by doing cardio work, building up lean muscle mass will aid in fat loss immensely. Why is this? The reason is muscle simply require a lot of calories to maintain its dense size and shape. A low calorie diet does not help with this cause due to the fact too few calories in a diet means your body will outright burn up muscle mass to make up for the deficit.

So, you want to eat meals that can help build muscle mass.

NOTE: THESE RECIPES ARE DESIGNED TO WORK IN CONJUNCTION WITH A WEIGHTLIFTING PROGRAM. You will not pack on muscle mass just by eating these foods alone, but if you are hitting the gym, they will help.

Chopped Steak With Mushroom Sauce

Ingredients:

Lean ground beef
Onion
Garlic
Salt & pepper
Brandy flavoring
Butter

(Those wishing to avoid red meat can use turkey instead)
Preheat an oven to about 400º.

Get a large sized bowl and mix in 2lbs of ground (LEAN!) beef. Add in about ¼ of a cup of onions and 2 tablespoons of garlic. One tablespoon of salt and pepper can be included. Mash everything up and then portion out about 8 burgers.

Put the burgers in the oven and allow then to cook for five or so minutes. Take the pan out of the oven and pour about two ounces of brandy on the burgers. Put the pan back in the oven allow the brandy flavoring to burn into the burgers.

Mix up two cups of beef stock, two full cups of quartered mushrooms, a teaspoon of thyme, a pinch of nutmeg, and a half tablespoon of rosemary. Add a tablespoon of butter to the mix. Put the contents on the burgers and cut them back in the oven for five minutes.

Serve the burgers and sauce over broccoli or any other vegetables. You can chop up the burgers beforehand if you wish.

Thai Spiced Chicken

Ingredients:

Chicken breasts
Thai red curry
Non or low-fat yogurt
Salt
Cilantro
Curry paste
Cucumber

Preheat an oven to about 375°f.

Cut six chicken breasts in half and place them in a shallow dish.

Put three tablespoons of Thai red curry paste, 4oz of nonfat or low-fat yogurt, and three tablespoons of cilantro in a blender. Blend everything up for a few minutes.

Season the mix with salt and then pour it over the chicken. Turn the chicken over repeatedly until it is evenly coated. Let the coating soak in for about ten minutes.

Roast the chicken in the oven for up to 40 minutes. You also have the option of barbecuing the chicken and this would take about 25 minutes.

Take 8 ounces of cold yogurt and a tablespoon of curry paste and blend it together. Chop up a four-inch piece of cucumber and mix it in with the yogurt. Serve this as a side dish with the cooked chicken.

Spicy Scrambled Eggs

Ingredients:

Half a dozen eggs
Olive oil
Cottage cheese
Red chili
Onion
Garlic
Mixed herbs

Add a little bit of olive oil to a frying pan to fully coat it.

Take a mixing bowl and add in about four egg whites and two whole eggs. Whisk until the six eggs are fully mixed.

Add in about ¼ of an onion along with one chopped up clove of garlic and a whole red chili.

Mix in 50 grams of cottage cheese and a pinch of mixed herbs. All of the contents will then need to be fully whisked.

Heat up the frying pan to a moderate level. Pour in the contents of the mixing bowl to the frying pan. Stir all the contents and scramble the eggs until they are cooked to the desired level.

Muscle Building Frozen Yogurt Peanut Butter Banana

Ingredients:

Greek yogurt
Banana
Natural peanut butter
Whey protein
Unsweetened cocoa or Cinnamon

Take a knife and cut up one large sized frozen banana. Put the chopped up banana pieces into a blender.

Pour into the blender about a half a cup of fat free Greek Yogurt.

Add two tablespoons of natural peanut butter to the blender.

Note: you really must use natural yogurt and peanut butter because the processed versions commonly sold would be among the worst selections for anyone interested in weight loss of muscle building.

A scoop of weight protein could be added if you want to really boost your muscle building potential. Chocolate or, of course, peanut butter flavored whey protein would be a wise and appropriate choice.

Unsweetened cocoa or Cinnamon could be put in the blender as well.

Blend the contents for a minute or more. You can eat it as is or you can place it in the refrigerator to cool.

Chapter Four

Fish Recipes to Lose Weight

Far too often, fish recipes are overlooked when it comes to suggesting diets for losing weight. There are a number of reasons why this is so. One would be cost. There is an assumption that most fish comes with high prices. The other would be the fact fish may spoil rather quickly if it is not cooked. Others will note that some fish dishes can require a lot of preparation making fish selections a bad choice for those that might be newbies to cooking.

Are all these facts correct?

The truth is not all fish dishes are expensive or complicated to make. Yes, fish can spoil quickly, but it can also be frozen. You also have to be aware that there are quite a number of easy fish dishes you can make even when you are relatively new to cooking.

Fish selections are packed with vitamins and nutrients. Cold-water fish are great for contributing to heart health. Yes, fish is low in calories, which makes fish choices perfect for those hoping to lose a few pounds.

There is also tremendous variety in the different types of fish dishes available. For those interested in weight loss, the following might prove incredibly helpful:

Spicy Stir Fry of Shrimp

Ingredients:

Shrimp
Noodles
Sesame oil
Chinese cabbage
Red and spring onions
Lime
Grated chili and ginger
Sweet chili sauce
Garlic
Soy and chili sauce

Boil a pot of water and put in two packages of prepared noodles. Allow the noodles to simmer for about four minutes. Drain the noodles and then top with one half of a teaspoon of sesame oil. Shake the noodles in the pan and let them wait on the side.

Peel and slice one red onion, shred a Chinese cabbage, and squeeze in the juice of a lime.

Place a large pan on the stove and heat it up. Add sesame oil to the pan. Once you see a small amount of smoke rising from the pan, put in one clove of garlic, a tablespoon of sweet chili sauce, and one tablespoon each of grated chili and ginger. Allow it to cook in the wok for about 30 seconds. Stir the contents.

Include the red onion, about four spring onions, and the shrimp. Stir-fry for about four minutes or until the shrimp are well cooked.

Include the Chinese cabbage, a teaspoon of lime juice, soy sauce and chili sauce. Toss in the noodles and about a cup of Chinese rice wine. Stir-fry for about four minutes and it will be ready to serve.

Salmon with Fresh Tomato Sauce

Ingredients:

Salmon fillets
Olive oil
Tomatoes
Tomato sauce
Balsamic vinegar
Salt & pepper

Heat up a griddle pan on the stove.

Take two salmon fillets and smother in one tablespoon of olive oil on the fillets.

Cook the salmon on the griddle for about three minutes. Rotate the salmon and let it cook for another three minutes.

At the same time, you should be preheating a frying pan.

Flip over the salmon. Let it cook for three minutes. Rotate the salmon and let it cook for another three minutes.

Heat another tablespoon of olive oil on the second

frying pan. Place two chopped up and skinned tomatoes in the pan. Pour a little balsamic vinegar on the tomatoes. A dash of salt and pepper can be added to the mix.

When serving the salmon, pour the tomato sauce on top of it.

Baked Cod with Chorizo & White Bean

Ingredients:

Cod
Shallot
Thyme
Chorizo
Great Northern Beans
Salt & pepper
Tomato sauce
Red wine
Grape tomatoes

Preheat your oven to about 425°F.

Place a medium saucepan on the stove at medium to high heat. In the saucepan, mix in one chopped up shallot, a teaspoon of thyme (also chopped) and two full ounces of chorizo. Stir in the pan for about a full minute.

Add one pint of grape tomatoes and a quarter of a cup of wine. Continue cooking until the wine is nearly evaporated and the tomatoes become soft. This could take about four minutes.

Stir a full 15-ounce can of great northern beans. Be sure

they are completely rinsed. Add a quarter teaspoon of salt.

Take the pan off the heat.

Put a little over one pound of cod on a baking pan and put a quarter teaspoon of salt and pepper on the fish.

Put the tomato sauce on top of the fish. Each fish fillet should get one cup of tomato sauce.

Pour one-quarter cup of wine on the baking pan. Put the fillets on the pan, cover the pan with foil and then put it in the oven.

Allow the fish to cook in the pan for about 20 minutes.

Southern Buttermilk Catfish Fillets

Ingredients:

Catfish fillets
Buttermilk
Cornmeal

Preheat a broiler at a moderate high level.

Spray cooking spray on a rack and place it on a baking sheet.

Cut four pieces of catfish fillets and put them in a small dish. Pour in one cup of buttermilk. Turn the fillets over allowing the buttermilk to soak in.

In the small dish, also stir in one-half cup of cornmeal, a half a teaspoon of paprika, salt, cayenne pepper, onion powder, and garlic powder.

Take the pieces of fish from the buttermilk. Shake off any excess buttermilk dripping from the fillets.

Put the fish in the cornmeal mixture and be sure that each side is thoroughly coated.

Take the fish and put them on the prepared rack. The rack and the fish then go in the broiler until done.

Fish Chowder

Ingredients:

Cod
Bacon
Celery
Russet potatoes
Thyme
Bay leaf
Low-fat milk

Heat a large saucepan on the stove and heat it to about medium level.

Take one strip of bacon and chop it up into bits. Put the bacon in the saucepan and stir it until it is totally crisp. Place it on the side when done.

In the pan with the bacon drippings, toss in one chopped celery stalk, a clove of garlic, and one small chopped onion. Stir these contents of the pan until they start to soften.

Pour in a cup of clam juice, and eight ounces of cubed cod or other fish selection. Dice about two cups of russet potatoes along with one teaspoon of chopped thyme and a single bay leaf. Turn the heat on the stove down a bit and place a cover on the saucepan. Allow it to simmer until the potatoes become soft. This might take about 10 minutes.

Remove about a third of the solids from the saucepan and mash them in a bowl with a fork or other implement. Put the mashed contents back in the saucepan and add in about two-thirds of a cup of low fat milk. Let the saucepan simmer.

Put two teaspoons of cornstarch and one tablespoon of water in a bowl and whisk them. Once your soup has come to a simmer, add in the cornstarch mix.

Stir up the soup consistently until it becomes thickened. This might take about a minute.

When served, add the bacon bits to the top of it.

Chapter Five

Raw Food Diet Recipes for the Daring

The Raw Food Diet definitely an acquired taste. Not everyone wishes to eat their meals uncooked. At one time in human history, such a preference was not always so avoidable. Today, many are learning to eat raw food once again because it can greatly aid in shedding unwanted and unnecessary pounds. Even if your goal is not to eat a purely raw food diet, you can still weave a few of these low calorie and healthy dishes into your weekly meal plans.

You can even just have them for dessert or as add-ons such as salsa. Here are a few of the top raw foods you can make. They are easy by default: all the steps for cooking them are removed from the equation!

A Simple Raw Pizza

Ingredients:

Olive oil
Water
Salt
Basil
Honey
Flax seeds
Almond
Sunflower seeds

This will require you to make the cheese, sauce and crust separately. Unlike other pizzas, there will be no need to cook any of these items,

Crust:

Put one-half a cup of water in a food processor with two tablespoons of olive oil, two teaspoons of dried basil, and three to four tablespoons of honey along with a small amount of salt. Turn the processor on and smooth all the contents out.

Take a mixing bowl and pour in three-quarters of flax seeds, two cups of almonds, and two cups of sunflower seeds. Pour in the processed water mixture into the bowl and mix everything up. Mash it with your hands to make a mound of dough.

Break the mound into four sections and roll them into a ball. Flatten the ball out on a teflex sheet. Put the sheet on a tray and place it in a dehydrator at 105 F for 10 hours. After the 10 hours are up, remove the sheet and place the tray back in the dehydrator for another 10 hours.

Sauce:

Take one cup of sun-dried tomatoes and soak them in water for two hours.

Chop up eight Roma tomatoes.

Put the chopped Roma tomatoes and the sun-dried tomatoes along with the soaked water in a blender.

In the blender, include one teaspoon of dried basil, a half a teaspoon of thyme, one teaspoon of dried oregano, two chopped cloves of garlic, three teaspoons of dried basil, two teaspoons of olive oil, and three pitted dates. Add one tablespoon of lemon juice and a dash of salt.

Blend until smooth.

Cheese:

Soak one cup of almonds in water for eight hours.

Put the almonds, one cup of water, 1 teaspoon of Celtic sea salt, two cloves of garlic, one-half a cup of raw cashews, and one tablespoon of lemon juice into a blender.

Once the mix is smooth and thick, take it out of the blender and place it in a glass bowl. Let it stand at room temperature.

The Pizza:

Put the pizza crust on a plate and pour the tomato sauce and cheese over it. Since this is a raw food selection, nothing is cooked.

Avocado, Banana, Chocolate Raw Pudding

Ingredients:

Bananas
Avocado
Cocoa powder

Take four very ripe bananas and put them in a blender.

Take one ripe avocado and peel and take the pit out. Put this in the blender with the bananas.

Add about one-quarter of a cup of cocoa powder to the blender.

Turn the blender on puree and turn the contents into a smooth pudding.

Pour the contents into a bowl and then place the bowl into the refrigerator and allow it to cool for about an hour.

Raw Avocado Mango Salsa
Peel, pit and dice an avocado in a small bowl.

Pour the juice from a single lime over the avocado. Mix

it up so the lime juice seeps in.

Peel, seed and dice a Mango, chop up one small red onion and chop a single habanero pepper. Add all this to the bowl with the avocado.

Add in tablespoon chopped fresh cilantro and a small amount of salt.

Mix all the contents up so they are evenly spread.

Chapter Six

Vegetarian and Vegan Recipes for Weight Loss

It would be a huge myth to prescribe to the notion that there is very little choice among selections of vegetarian and vegan recipes. It also would be a myth that all vegetarian food selections are served raw. There are quite a number of unique, innovative and appealing vegetarian dishes available for make. Yes, the array of vegetarian desserts is vast as well.

Of course, vegetables are very low in calories and very high in nutrients and vitamins. For those wishing to lose weight, vegetarian recipes can prove very helpful. Vegetables, by their very nature, are low in calories. That alone is something to be mindful of when you want a diet you need to lose weight. Also, you do not always want to burden your metabolism with meat and poultry. It takes a lot to break such foods down and that can leave you feeling a little too weak for workouts or exercise.

Do you have to eat all your meals vegetarian style in

order to shed pounds? No, you do have the ability to mix and match. Some may opt to eat one-third of their meals vegetarian style as a great way of cutting pounds.

Here are a few of those excellent vegetarian recipes to take advantage of:

Grilled Tofu with Ratatouille Vegetables

Ingredients:

Tofu
Eggplants
Zucchini
Dry rose wine
Orange juice
Herbs de Provence
Organic vegetable broth
Olive Oil
Olive paste
Ground black pepper
Kosher salt
Red bell pepper
Garlic
Sweet onion
Tomato
Thyme
Basil

Preheat the grill to about medium heat levels.

Pour one cup of organic vegetable broth, a half a cup of dry rose wine, a half a cup of orange juice, two teaspoons of dried herbs de Provence into a medium high heated saucepan. Allow the contents to come to a boil. After about ten minutes, the contents should become somewhat syrupy and evaporate to about one-third of a cup.

Take the sauce away from the heat and allow it to cool. Mix in and stir in One teaspoon of olive oil, one tablespoon of olive paste, a quarter teaspoon of ground black pepper, and one-half a teaspoon of kosher salt. Add four minced cloves of garlic.

Take a full package of tofu and cut it into 8 slices. Put the tofu along with three eggplants and zucchini cut into four slices, one large red bell pepper, one sweet onion cut into slices, and four tomatoes on the heated grill.

Use a brush to apply about half of the juice mixture over the tofu and the vegetables and let it grill for four full minutes. After the four minutes are up, turn the tofu and the vegetables over. Brush the over half of the sauce over them. Allow them to cook for another four minutes or until golden brown.

Add about one tablespoon of fresh thyme, one tablespoon of fresh parsley, and a tablespoon of chopped basil.

Slow Cooker Vegetarian Chili

Ingredients:

Black bean soup
Kidney beans
Garbanzo
Tomatoes
Vegetarian baked beans
Gene bell pepper
Celery
Garlic
Onion
Kernel corn
Oregano, basil, parsley, and chili powder

Place one full can of black bean soup along with one can of kidney beans in a slow cooker. The kidney beans must be rinsed and drained well first. Also, rinse and drain garbanzo beans and add them to the slow cooker. A can of vegetarian baked beans and a can of chopped tomatoes in puree are also placed in the cooker. Drain an entire can of whole kernel corn and include it as well.

Chop up an entire onion, one green bell pepper, two cloves of garlic, and two stalks of celery and add them to the slow cooker.

Put one tablespoon of chili powder, one tablespoon of dried parsley, dried oregano and dried basil.

Put the slow cooker on high and let it cook for about two hours.

Lemon-Scented Oven-Roasted Winter Squash

Ingredients:

Winter squash
Olive oil
Sea salt
Lemon

Preheat an oven to about 375 degrees.

Cut up a winter squash into about three cups of cubes about one inch in size.

Place the cubes in a small mixing bowl.

Add to the mixing bowl enough olive oil to cover the cubes. Sprinkle a small amount of sea salt.

Pour in a generous amount of maple flavored brown rice syrup.

Include the grated zest of one full lemon and the juice of half a lemon.

Stir all the contents of the bowl until the cubes are completely covered in the mix.

Place the marinated squash cubes on a baking dish. Cover the dish and place in the oven to bake for about 45 minutes. Take off the cover and put it back in the oven for a short time in order to brown the edges.

When served, it can be sprinkled with lemon juice.

Zucchini-Corn Cannelloni

Ingredients:

Olive oil
Onion
Garlic
Sage
Oregano
Fire-roasted tomatoes
Balsamic vinegar
Salt & pepper

Sauce:

Heat one and a half teaspoons of olive oil in a saucepan at about medium heat.

Add one-half a cup of chopped onion to the oil in the pan and sauté until the onions are soft.

Add one clove of mixed garlic, a half a teaspoon of rubbed sage, and a half a teaspoon of oregano.

Include one full can of diced fire-roasted tomatoes and one teaspoon of balsamic vinegar and a little bit of salt and pepper.

Cover the pan and lower the heat. Let it simmer for about ten minutes. Afterwards, place the sauce in a blender and puree it.

Cannelloni:

Ingredients:

Zucchini
Onions
Olive oil
Zucchini
Corn kernel

Heat one tablespoon of olive oil in a pan at about medium heat.

One and one-half cups of chopped onions can be put in the pan and sautéed for about ten minutes.

After sautéing the onions, add in one and one half a cup of zucchini that has been diced and one-half a cup of frozen corn kernels.

Turn the heat up on the stove and sauté the new mix for about five minutes.

Mince two cloves of garlics and put it in the pan along with a half a teaspoon of rubbed sage. Stir up the contents.

Take the pan off the stove and allow it to cool a little. Add and stir four tablespoons of Parmesan cheese, a pinch of ground nutmeg, and one full cup of low fat ricotta cheese.

Boil a pot of water with salt in it. Cook a half dozen lasagna noodles (no cook variety) until the noodles soften. Drain the noodles and place them in cool water then drain them again. Put them on a cutting board and cut them in half width wise.

Cooking it:

Preheat oven to about 350°.

Put about half a cup of tomato sauce on a baking dish.

Put three tablespoons of the zucchini mix in the middle of a halved noodle. Then, roll the noodle and repeat this process with all the noodles you have.

Pour all the sauce left over on top of the Cannelloni in

the baking dish. Cover it with about one-half a cup of low fat mozzarella.

Bake for a little over 20 minutes. The dish should be baked until the sauce is bubbly and the cheese is melted.

This dish can be served hot or cold.

Mixed-Grain Tabbouleh with Roasted Eggplant, Chickpeas, and Mint

Ingredients:

Eggplants (3)
Salt & pepper
Olive oil
Salted water
Bulgur
Cilantro
Quinoa

Preheat an oven to 450°.

Spray no stick spray on a baking sheet.

Spread three cubed eggplants onto the baking sheet. You may wish to add a little no stick spray to the cubes. Add about one-quarter teaspoon of salt and pepper. Top the eggplants with one and one-half tablespoon of olive oil.

Roast the eggplant in the oven for about 20 minutes. Take the sheet out and turn the eggplant cubes around. Roast for another 10 minutes. Take it out of the oven and let it cool.

Boil a pot of salted water. Boil a quarter cup of bulgur for five minutes. Then, add two-thirds of a cup of quinoa that has been rinsed and drained. Boil for another 12 minutes or so. Drain it all out and move it to a large bowl.

Mix in two-thirds of a cup of chopped mints and one-third a cup of chopped cilantro into grains. Mix it all with the eggplants and a cup of halved tomatoes.

Pour in and whisk two tablespoons of lemon juice in a bowl. Add two tablespoons of olive oil, a half a teaspoon of salt, and a half a teaspoon of pepper in the bowl. Marinate one cup of cooked chickpeas and a half a cup of chopped red onions for about 15 minutes.

Take the chickpea mixture and fold it into grains. Garnish these with mint sprigs.

Chapter Seven

Paleolithic Diet Recipes: Turning Back the Clock.... A Lot

It is not exactly a secret that the diet world is one that is known for its high volume of fads. Sometimes, a new fad is actually an old diet that has reemerged. After a number of years. What makes the Paleo diet an extreme form of this would be the fact it is a diet from a very old era...the Paleolithic one!

Yes, our modern ancestors of the caveman days were able to survive in the harshest of conditions. One reason they were able to survive is their diet was free of a lot of the troubling food selections we commonly eat in the modern era.

There is no reason we cannot duplicate the Paleo diet in modern times. All we have to do is take the steps to cut back on eating a lot of the bad foods that have a tendency to pack on weight and make us sick. This diet is one that helps cut back on those troubling food selections. In turn, you cut back on a lot of calories and a ton of unwanted processed ingredients.

But, is this diet little more than another fad?

Some might think the word fad is a very bad one. Honestly, a fad does not automatically mean a diet is a poor one. Rather, it means that the diet gains appeal from the masses for a short time only to be discarded later. You can let the masses do whatever it is they want. If you stick with a good diet, you will find it will work for you. The following are a few Paleo diet recipes you might find very helpful as far as cutting calories and changing up a few of your weekly meals.

Remember, this is a grain free, all-natural diet. You would have a hard time not losing weight on it. Some of the selection might admittedly be very acquired tastes.

Steak Tartar

Ingredients:

Beef tenderloin sirloin steak
Red wine or alternative (stock)
Tabasco
Garlic
Salt
Curry powder

Take two and a half pound of beef tenderloin sirloin steak and chop it up into cubes. Put the cubes in a food processor and puree the meat. Once it has been ground up properly, put the meat in a bowl.

In the bowl, mix in four tablespoons of red wine (or stock) and three-quarters of a teaspoon of Tabasco.

Mince up three cloves of garlic and add it to the bowl of ground beef.

Mix in one teaspoon each of salt and curry powder and two teaspoons of dry mustard.

Mix up all the ingredients in the meat together.

Place the bowl in the refrigerator and allow it to cool for a couple hours.

Once cooled, the dish can be served.

Pork (or lamb) Chops and Sauerkraut

Ingredients:

Pork chops
Sauerkraut
Apples
Ketchup
Honey
Garlic salt & pepper

Preheat an oven to about 325 F.

Take four to six pork chops and douse them in olive oil until they are brown.

Put one pound of sauerkraut and two fully grated apples in a baking pan along with one-third of a cup of ketchup and two tablespoons of honey.

Add in a desired amount of garlic salt and pepper.

Top the mix of sauerkraut with the browned pork chops and place them in the oven.

Bake the pork chops until done which may be one or two hours.

Lamb in Red Wine Sauce

Ingredients:

Leg of lamb
Salt & pepper
Olive oil
Red wine or alternative (stock)
Garlic cloves
Celery
Onions
Wine vinegar

Take one full leg of lamb and cut all the fat off it. Apply salt and pepper to the lamb.

Heat about two tablespoons of olive oil on the stove. After heating it, fry the lamb leg in the olive oil until it is completely browned. Be sure all fat is drained off before moving to the next step in the process.

The lamb must be placed in a Dutch oven. About two bottles of good red wine (or stock) must be added to the lamb.

A flavoring mix is to be made and this is a combination of two peeled onions, two celery sticks, about a dozen peeled garlic gloves, and a bit of salt and pepper. Put these in the Dutch oven with the lamb so the lamb can be flavored.

Once the lamb has been browned, take it out of the Dutch oven. Scoop one tablespoon of fat out of the Dutch oven and put it in a bold. Dice up two carrots, two diced onions, and two diced celery stalks. Sauté them in the Dutch oven until they are brown. Put the lamb back in the Dutch oven with this mix.

A little wine vinegar and salt should be added to the lamb.

Place a cover over the pot and allow it to cook in an oven at about 430 degrees.

The lamb will need to be turned about twice while it is cooked to avoid it burning or cooking unevenly. There will need to be a bit of patience here since the lamb will have to cook for about four hours to that it becomes very flaky when the time comes to eat it.

When you remove the lamb from the oven, you can drain the sauce from the pan and serve the lamb with it.

Vanilla Blueberry Omelet

Ingredients:

Eggs (2)
Vanilla extract
Blueberries
Coconut oil

Place two eggs in a bowl and add one teaspoon of vanilla extract.

A small frying pan can be place on the stove and heated at medium level.

Put a quarter cup of blueberries in the frying pan as it heats and mash them until blueberry juice comes out.

Place another pan on the stove and smear a little coconut oil on the pan. Allow the pan to heat.

Pour the eggs into the pan and scramble a little. Allow the eggs to three-quarters cook and then scramble again. The eggs on the side of the pan will slowly become crisp and when they do, add the remaining blueberries to the eggs.

Fold the omelet over the blueberries. Cook a short bit and then remove the omelet from the pan.

Top with the blueberry mix that was cooked in the other pan. Serve.

Chapter Eight

Breakfast Recipes for Weight Loss

It has been said that breakfast is the most important meal of the day. This is certainly true because you do what to get a large amount of (good) calories early in the morning. You can then taper down your calorie intake during the rest of the day.

The problem here is so many breakfast meals are loaded with calories and refined carbohydrates. A stack of waffles with fatty butter and sugary maple syrup or an omelet with extremely fatty cheese and pork byproducts will pack on a lot of unwanted pounds.

Unfortunately, many will eat such selections because they are absolutely unaware of good breakfast choices that can be perfect for losing weight. The following recipes can certainly help with keeping weight down and supplying the body with the right amount of good nutrients that make a breakfast perfect.

Do not make the mistake of assuming breakfast should never be part of a well-rounded, healthy diet. Then again, once you review a few of these breakfast selections, you probably will be enthused to give them a try. Afterwards, you might never go back to the old school, sugary and fatty breakfast selections that are way too common.

Oats and Raspberry Natural Pancakes

You have two different components to this recipe. The first would be the oats pancakes and the other would be the raspberry compote.

The Oats Pancake Mix:

Ingredients:

Egg
Buttermilk
Wheat flour
Cane sugar
Baking soda
Cinnamon
Salt

Pour two cups of buttermilk and one egg in a bowl. Mix one and a half cup of oats, a half a cup of whole wheat flour, a tablespoon of sugar, flour, and one small teaspoon of baking soda and a half teaspoon of cinnamon and salt in a small bowl. Then, pour the wet milk and egg mix into the dry bowl and mix it all together. Let this stand for about 12 minutes.

Raspberry Compote:

Ingredients:

Raspberries
Organic maple syrup
Cinnamon

Take a small bowl and add two full cups of fresh raspberries to it. Add two tablespoon of natural, organic maple syrup to the bowl along with one teaspoon of cinnamon. Mix thoroughly and pour into a saucepan. Allow it to simmer on the stove at medium heat until the berries are three-quarters melted. Once this is done, the saucepan can be removed from the stove and allowed to cool.

Cooking the Oats Pancakes:

Heat a griddle or frying pan that has been coated with no stick spray. Pour the oat pancake batter on the pan and allow them to cook until the bubble. When they do, you can flip them over and cook (brown) the other side.

When finished, pour the compote on top of the oat cakes and serve.

Oatmeal-Rhubarb Porridge

Ingredients:

Almond or Soy Milk
Orange juice
Rhubarb
Cinnamon
Salt
Brown sugar
Organic maple syrup
Nuts

Place a saucepan on the kitchen counter and pour in one and one half cups of almond or soymilk along with one-half of a cup of orange juice. A pinch of salt, a half a teaspoon of cinnamon and a cup of chopped rhubarb are to be added to the pan. Place the pan on the stove at medium high.

After the contents boil, you lower the heat and allot it to slowly cook for another five minutes as you stir it. Once the oats and rhubarb have softened, you can take it off the stove, cover it, and allow it to cook for five minutes or so.

Two or three tablespoons of brown sugar or natural,

organic maple syrup and non-salted nuts can be then put in the porridge.

Vegetable and Ham Breakfast Slice

Eggs (4)
Low-fat milk
Ham slices
Carrot
Scallions
Sweet Corn
Organic flour

Preheat and over to about 350 degrees Fahrenheit and spray nonstick on a baking pan.

Pour one cup of low fat milk in a small bowl. Crack four eggs into the bowl and whisk thoroughly. A pinch of salt and pepper can be added.

On a cutting board, chop up two slices of ham into small chunks. Grate a small carrot and slice up two scallions. Drain one-half of a cup of sweet corn and put it into the mixing bowl with the milk and egg combo. Add the ham, carrots and scallions to the bowl and mix up thoroughly.

Pour a half a cup of organic flour into the bowl and mix everything together.

Pour the contents of the bowl on the pan and then place

it in the oven for about 35 minutes or until fully cooked.

When done, cut into square slices and serve.

Low Fat Mushroom Omelet

Ingredients:

Eggs (4)
Low-fat milk
Salt & pepper
Onion
Olive oil
Mushrooms

Crack four eggs into a mixing bowl and add about a half a cup of low fat milk. A pinch of salt and pepper can be tossed in for further taste.

A frying pan will need to be preheated on the oven at medium level.

Chop up one-half a small onion and put it in the frying pan. Drizzle about two teaspoons of olive oil over the onions. Stir the two so the onions are sautéed. This might take about four minutes.

Take about five and a half ounces of sliced mushrooms and place them in the frying pan. Stir and sauté them as well until they are softened. The mushrooms should be fully cooked after four minutes. Once they are cooked, take them out of the pan and put them in a bowl on the side. Allow the onions and mushrooms to cool.

As soon as they have cooled down, you can add the eggs/milk mix to the bowl and stir everything together up.

Preheat another pan (or the same one) on the stove. Some olive oil can be used to keep the eggs from sticking on the pan. Regular cooking spray will work as well.

Pour the egg/mushroom/onion mix into the pan. Let it cook for a minute or two and flip it over. Allow the omelet to fully cook and then serve.

Eggs Benedict Italian Style

Ingredients:

Eggs (8)
Wheat muffins (4)
Parmesan cheese
Tomato
Zucchini
Shallot
White vinegar
Balsamic vinegar
Basil
Salt & pepper
Garlic clove
Olive Oil
Water

Put a large skillet on the stove and fill it with water. Boil the water and add about a quarter of a cup of white vinegar.

In another skillet, heat up two teaspoons of olive oil. Toss in one fully minced clove of garlic and an entire shallot. Cook the contents for a little over a minute stirring all the while.

Dice up two zucchini and three tomatoes. Place them in the pan and mix them up with the shallot and garlic. You may wish to let it cook for about 12 minutes or until the zucchini softens. Take the pan off the stove and mix in three tablespoons of basil, one tablespoon of balsamic vinegar and a little salt and pepper, draw down the temperature of the boiling water allowing it to simmer. Crack and add eight eggs into the water and allow them to cook as soft or as hard as you want them to be. Take them out of the water and allow them to drain on a towel.

Toast four whole-wheat English muffins and put them on a plate. This will give you eight halves of a muffin...one for each of the eight eggs. Put the eggs on the muffin with the vegetables and some Parmesan cheese and serve.

Chapter Nine

Desserts for the Diet Conscious

If your goal is to lose weight, you probably are under the assumption that desserts are something you should stay away from. In truth, high calorie desserts that are low in nutrients and packed with fats and processed sugar are something you should stay away from when you want to shed pounds.

This is true, but there are a few lower calorie desserts you can add to your daily meals. Many of these desserts are natural and devoid of processed ingredients. Certainly, you cannot eat these in an indulgent manner. You must always be mindful of your daily calorie count. However, if you are watching your calories and remain very active during the day, you will find one or two dessert items can make a nice addition to your daily meal.

There is another benefit to have a dessert now and then: it can keep you from feeling that you are deriving yourself of all things enjoyable. When you feel deprived, you might quit your diet and go on a binge. Rather than do this, you might want to have a dessert now and then that really is not all that bad for your weight loss goals.

The key to it not being so bad would be selecting desserts designed for those on a diet. Are they many? There are actually quite a few. Here is a brief look at some of them:

Cottage Cheese Dessert (and Breakfast) Pancakes

Ingredients:

Egg
Low-fat milk
Cottage cheese
Frozen berries
Vegetable oil
Flour
Salt
Natural sugar
Yogurt
Water

Toss one cup of flour in a bowl. (You may wish to buy low carb flour or organic flour)

Add a pinch of salt.

Whisk one egg and a single cup of low fat milk in the bowl. Include one teaspoon of vanilla extract.

Once the above is whisked, mix and whisk in one-half a cup of low fat cottage cheese. Do not worry if the mix is less than even.

Put the mix in the fridge to cool.

Put a saucepan on the stove and heat it. One cup of frozen berries should be put in the saucepan along with a tablespoon of natural sugar and a half a cup of water. Allow this mix to simmer on the stove for a little over one minute. Once the contents take on a thicker texture, the heat can be turned off and the pan can be put on the side allowing the sauce to cool.

Heat a frying pan at medium and add a little vegetable oil to make sure the pancakes do not stick.

Pour the cottage cheese pancake mix to the pan and cook until they are browned. Flip them as you would any other pancakes...when they bubble.

The pancakes are served on a plate with the homemade berry sauce and/or spoonful's of berry-flavored yogurt.

If serving for breakfast, you would not add any berry sauce or yogurt.

Honey-Lime Fruit Cup

Ingredients:

A selection of your favorite fruits
Lime
Honey

Select your own personal favorite fruits and mix them into a serving bowl. The amount of the fruit should be one cup.

Take one lime and juice it and zest it.

Mix in one-half a teaspoon of both lime zest and lime juice in a bowl and whisk it with one-half a tablespoon of honey. The end result should be a seamless mixture.

Pour the mixture over the fruit in the bowl and mix it up nicely.

Chocolate and Raspberry Pudding

Ingredients:

Egg
Organic cocoa
Natural cane sugar
Self Raising Flour
Skim of low-fat milk
Low-fat yogurt
Margarine
Brown sugar
Salt
Water

Preheat your over to about 325 F.

Place 200 grams of Self Raising Flour in a bowl with three tablespoons of organic cocoa, a pinch of salt, and a half a cup of natural cane sugar. Mix all the contents together.

Put a small pot on a stove at a moderate level of heat and mix in one-quarter cup of cane sugar, a full cup of raspberries, and one-quarter a cup of water, and allow it to simmer for over five minutes. Stir it slightly. After the five minutes is up, put the sauce on the side.

Whisk one egg, a quarter cup of skim or low fat milk, and two tablespoons of margarine. Add the raspberry mix to it.

In a small bowl, make a sauce mix of two tablespoons of both brown sugar and cocoa and two cups of warm water. This makes the cake sauce.

This new cake mix will be put in a baking pan. Dribble the sauce over it. It then goes into the oven for about 45 minutes.

The cake can be served with the low fat yogurt of your choice.

Apple and Blueberry Cobbler

Ingredients:

Apples (4)
Blueberries
Eggs (2)
Caster sugar
Salt
Cinnamon
Margarine
Milk
Flour

An oven must be preheated to 350F

Core and peel four fresh apples. Organic apples may be preferable. Cut the apples into chunks

The apples along with two cups of fresh blueberries should be placed in an oven dish. Cover them loosely with one-quarter a cup of caster sugar and a pinch of salt and cinnamon. Mix the fruit up a bit.

In a small bowl, sift one and a half cups of flour and one teaspoon of baking powder.

Take a beater and beat and smooth three-quarters sugar and four tablespoons of margarine. Once it has been smoothed, add in a teaspoon of vanilla extract. Beat some more. An egg will go into the mix and beaten until smooth. Then, a second egg will be added and the mix will be beaten until smooth.

Take one-third a cup of flour and beat it in the mix until smooth. One-third of a cup of milk will be incorporated and beat until smooth. Repeat this step two more times.

Using a spoon and not a beater, mix in three-quarters a cup of blueberries. Do not mash them.

The new mixture you have created can now be mixed evenly with the fruit mix that was previously made. Afterwards, place it in the oven and allow it to cook for a full hour.

Appendix I:

A Five-Day Sample Meal Plan

How can you plan your weekday meals? It is not hard. Here is an example of a simple five-day meal plan you can examine as a sample of a good diet for weight loss.

Note: The bulk of these days reflect a daily calorie count of less than 2,000. This might be very low for some depending on their current weight and how much they want to shed. For those wishing to maintain a certain desired amount of daily calories, it is best to make a solid log of what you eat each day and look up the number of calories in each food item. This way, you will always be on top of your calorie consumption.

Monday

Breakfast: Whole Wheat Pancakes
Lunch: Tuna Salad with No Mayonnaise on Lettuce with Light Oil
Dinner: Vegetable Lasagna

Tuesday

Breakfast: Fruit Cup with Small Whole Grain Muffin
Lunch: Low Carb Lean Hamburger Wrap: Lean Grilled Beef with Lettuce, Tomato and Onion Wrapped in Lettuce.
Dinner: Pork tenderloin stuffed mushroom and onion and a cup of mixed vegetable and a green salad.
Dessert: Vegan Chocolate Pudding

Wednesday
Breakfast: Italian Style Eggs Benedict
Lunch: Ham and Cheese Sandwich on Whole Wheat Bread
Dinner: Baked Salmon with brown rice

Thursday

Breakfast: One-half cup homemade granola
Lunch: Turkey Burger with a Grilled Tomato on a Bed of Lettuce
Dinner: Marinated Chicken with vegetables
Dessert: Yogurt Pancakes Topped with Fruit.

Friday

Breakfast: Mushroom, Ham and Egg White Omelet.
Lunch: Grilled Fish with Brown Rice or Noodles.

Dinner: Baked Chicken with Lemon and Mixed Vegetables.

Conclusion

Final Words that are Not So Final

Hopefully, this cook book has given you quite a bit of food for thought... and for breakfast, lunch, dinner, and dessert.

In all seriousness, the selections found in this cookbook are intended to help you lose weight. They are low in calories and high in nutritional value. Rather than provide an entire book of one type of recipe, a whole host of different ones were offered so you will not become bored with the selections placed in front of you.

It does bear mentioning that even the very best food will cause you to gain weight if you eat too much of it. Losing weight is based on a calorie deficit. That means you have to eat less than the amount of calories you burn. No, you need not starve yourself because that would be self-defeating and do little more than slow your metabolism down. Remember what we said earlier about how crash diets can cause binge eating? It is true! So, you want to stay away from such risky diets. Eat healthy and eat in moderation. Combine this with a proper amount of exercise and you can lose weight.

Best of all, you can lose weight while eating an amazing selection and array of food.

Enjoy!

Section 2: Low Carb Diet

Low calorie diet is a general phrase that can have different meanings. Anyone can eat smaller portions of the same foods they are already consuming, but this doesn't adequately justify a low calorie diet. What you eat makes a huge difference in getting the most out of any type of diet. Advertising trends can misrepresent the true meaning of a low calorie diet, while staying within certain truthful perimeters. This book is designed to bring focus on true low calorie diets, that introduce you to a new way of life. Being stronger, healthier and having more energy, is the goal of a successful low calorie diet.

There will be misconceptions addressed, as you read through the chapters. Facts about preservatives, sugar, grains and drinks, will awaken your thoughts about what you are feeding yourself, and your family. The truth is, a low calorie diet is not just for losing weight, but learning how all foods have a direct effect on your body. Just as you know that cigarettes and large amounts of alcohol are harmful, habits of eating certain foods can weaken you immune system, slow down metabolism, and cause fatty tissue to form in your arteries and veins.

You will also find delicious recipes that are just right for stepping into your new life. If you wish to shed a few pounds, mix and match the recipes and portions, according to the carbs. With each recipe made from low-carb foods, and under 500 calories each, the choices are huge.

Why Calorie Counting is a Lie

Keeping calories low should not involve taking out a book and writing down every calorie of food you eat. That gets real boring, real fast. You simply need to know what types of foods can easily be burned off and which ones, cannot. One of the highest forms of calories that is difficult to unload, is sugar. Look at any label and you will see this word.

According to the American Heart Association, no more than 100 calories of sugar should make up a grown woman's diet in one day. This amounts to 6 teaspoons. For a man, 150 calories, or 9 teaspoons, should be the limit. One bowl of whole-grain cereal with milk, contains as much as 9 teaspoons of sugar.

While this may seem downhearted, it gets even worse. Preservatives play a very important role in adding empty calories and high carbs. Take, for example, a box of macaroni and cheese. You may feel that you are being frugal in selecting a product that has cheese, grain, and vitamins, not to mention a shelf life of a year, but here is the ugly truth. Preservatives contain corn syrup, hydrogenated oil, nitrates or sulfates. While consumption of these ingredients can give you a sensation of fullness, they are very difficult for the digestive system to process. Feeling sluggish, developing heart burn and producing fat, are three real symptoms of consuming processed foods. While the package calories may read, 400 calories per serving, is doesn't tell you that these calories are close to impossible to burn off.

You can make it a habit of counting calories, but unless you start with foods that are good for your body, consuming a low carb diet, will be in vein.

Chapter 1: Rise and Shine with a Fortified Breakfast

Crunchy Maple Grape Nuts

Description

Breakfast should contain energy-packed foods to jump start your day. However, in the hustle and bustle of preparing for the day, many people grab a box of cereal. Instead of breaking this habit, keep your own homemade varieties on hand. Low calorie and delicious, these recipes will give your family the right mix of vitamins in a low carb diet. Make ahead and store in airtight containers.

Yields: 12 Servings

Ingredients

3 cups whole wheat flour
1/2 cup barley flour
1/3 cup oat flour
1/3 cup toasted wheat germ
1/2 cup brown sugar

1/2 teaspoon salt
2 teaspoons baking soda
2 teaspoons maple flavoring
1/4 cup heated honey or maple syrup
1/2 cup low-fat milk
2 teaspoons cinnamon

Instructions

1. Warm oven to 325 degrees.

2. Sift and blend dry ingredients

3. In a separate bowl, beat the liquid ingredients together.

4. Stir liquid ingredients into dry ingredients.

5. If the mixture is too watery, work in additional flour.

6, Spread on 2 or 3 baking sheets and bake for 10-15 minutes. After baking, allow to cool, then break up any large clumps and return to oven for an additional 10 minutes.

7. Cool and store in air-tight container.

Healthy Honey Oat Cereal

Description

Here is another version of homemade cereal for those that love to wake up their mouths with lots of crunch and flavor. Nuts, raisins and sweet natural ingredients make this breakfast cereal a great kick start to the day.

Yields: 12 Servings

Ingredients

4 1/2 cups rolled oats
6 Tablespoons sunflower seeds
12 Tablespoons sliced almonds
6 Tablespoons chopped pecans
6 Tablespoons raisins
6 Tablespoons honey
1/4 teaspoon cinnamon
1/4 teaspoon maple extract

Instructions

1. Warm oven to 325 degrees.

2. Place a small pan over a larger pan of boiling water

and add the honey, cinnamon and extract. Heat just until well mixed.

3. Spread baking sheet with aluminum foil and combine all other ingredients (except raisins). You may want to use a baking pan that has a slight lip around the sides, or raise up the edges of the foil to keep dry ingredients from falling off.

4. Using your hands, or a large wooden spoon, mix well, the dry ingredients.

5. Add the honey mixture and coat as much of the dry ingredients as you can.

6. Spread the mixture evenly over the pan and bake for 15 minutes.

7. Remove from oven and let cool. Do not worry if your cereal does not appear crunchy. This comes once it has cooled.

9. After cooling, mix in the raisins and store in an airtight container.

French Toast Strawberry Dippers

Description

Getting kids to the breakfast table is a tough chore. Usually running late, they will grab a finger food, like a doughnut or other gluten-filled treat. Have these quick dippers ready to reach for as they hit the door, and know that they are getting good taste and healthy energy.

Yields: 4 Servings

Ingredients

- 8 slices low-carb sandwich white bread
- 4 Tablespoons softened cream cheese
- 6 fresh, sliced strawberries
- 3 large eggs
- 1/4 cup low-fat milk
- 1 Tablespoon butter
- 1/2 cup maple syrup
- 1/4 cup no-sugar strawberry jam

Instructions

1. Spread cream cheese on 4 slices of bread.

2. Line the cream cheese topping with the sliced strawberries.

3. Top with a bread slice to make a sandwich.

4. In a bowl, mix together the eggs and milk.

5. Use 1/2 of the butter to lightly grease a griddle or skillet and heat on medium.

6. Dip the sandwiches into the egg batter, one at a time, and place in the warmed griddle or skillet.

7. Cook the bread on each side until golden brown. Add remaining butter, if needed.

8. Remove each sandwich, pat with paper towels and cut into 4 long sections.

9. Combine the syrup and jam and heat in a microwave for 30 seconds.

10.Remove and stir well.

11.Place the tasty toast sections in a bread basket, beside the dip, and watch them disappear.

Breakfast Egg Muffins

Description

Use the weekend to cook up a filling and healthy egg breakfast for the day ahead. It will soon become a tradition of a starting a free day, just right, with plenty to go around.

Yields: 8 Servings

Ingredients

8 eggs
½ cup Swiss or Cheddar cheese
½ cup milk
¼ cup chopped onion
¼ cup chopped mushrooms
¼ cup green pepper
¼ cup chopped tomatoes
2 Tablespoons butter
4 plain bagels
8 stale pieces of bread

Instructions

1. Lay out the pieces of bread and cut out the middle in

the shape of a circle. This will serve as a pattern for cooking your egg mixture.

2. In a bowl, whisk the eggs and milk together.

3. Blend in the onion, mushrooms, green pepper and tomatoes.

4. Melt 1 Tablespoon butter in a large skillet and arrange the bread patterns.

5. Pour the egg mixture in the center of each bread pattern, lower heat and cover.

6. After about 4 minutes, remove the cover and sprinkle each round egg with cheese.

7. Add extra butter if needed to keep the bottoms from sticking.

7. Turn off heat and recover skillet.

8. Toast ½ bagel and place on a plate.

9. Carefully remove each egg and peel away the outer bread.

10. Place the round egg on top of the bagel, discarding the bread.

Serve with fresh fruit or a glass of juice.

Cinnamon Raisin Muffins

Description

Nothing can compare to fresh, homemade muffins, right from the oven. These treats will satisfy your craving for bread and sweets, but actually give you less than 150 calories each. Vary the ingredients and have a different selection of muffins each week.

Yields: 12 Servings

Ingredients

1 ½ cups flour
1 ½ teaspoons baking powder
½ teaspoon baking soda
¼ cup butter, refrigerated
1 egg
¼ cup sour cream
¼ cup milk
¼ cup raisins
2 Tablespoons sugar, or sugar substitute
1 teaspoon cinnamon

Instructions

1. Heat oven to 400 degrees F.

2. Combine flour, baking powder and baking soda in large bowl.

3. Cut in the butter until coarse crumbs form.

4. Make a well in the center.

5. In a small bowl, beat the egg, then add the sour cream, milk, raisins, sugar and cinnamon, blending thoroughly.

6. Pour the egg mixture in the center of the flour and mix well.

7. Take a muffin pan and either line with paper muffin holders, or grease lightly.

8. Fill each cup 2/3 full.

9. Bake for 15 minutes, or until browned.

Apple butter or fruit preserves can be used to spread on each muffin.

Asparagus and Mushroom Omelet

Description

This dish makes a meaty and tasty meal for not only breakfast, but lunch, as well. With only 5 grams of carbohydrates and 21 grams of protein, per serving, you will pick up extra energy and not get hungry through the course of the day.

Yields: 4 Servings

Ingredients

8 eggs
8 Tablespoons water
12 stalks fresh asparagus
1 cup sliced mushrooms
1 cup low-fat mozzarella cheese

Instructions

1. In a large skillet, add an inch of water and bring to a boil.

2. Add the asparagus, in two or three different sections, and cook uncovered, just until tender-crisp. Remove and

pat dry.

3. Using a large bowl, whisk the eggs and water.

4. Prepare a large skillet by melting 1 Tablespoon butter

.

5. When butter reaches a sizzle over medium-high heat, add ½ of the egg mixture.

6. Cook until the bottom of the egg mixture sets.

7. Carefully lift up the edges with a spatula and allow the uncooked portion to flow out and cook.

8. Once the top is cooked thoroughly, add the asparagus, mushrooms and cheese, and fold into a sandwich with part of the egg.

9. Remove the omelet and cut in half. Repeat with the rest of the egg mixture.

Chapter 2: Lunchtime Recipes for Afternoon Energy

Eggs, Lox and Caramelized Onions on Bagel

Description

Afternoons do not have to be a battle with fatigue and a sluggish feeling. Allow your mid-day meal to recharge your body with fulfilling foods that bring nutrition to your organs and pep up your blood flow. You'll never miss the calories, but you will enjoy missing that afternoon slump that used to slow you down.

Yields: 4 Servings

Ingredients

4 teaspoons butter
1 sliced onion
8 eggs
2 Tablespoons heavy cream
4 ounces lox
4 toasted buns

Instructions

1. Melt 2 teaspoons butter in a skillet, add sliced onions, and cook over medium heat for 8-10 minutes, or until golden brown. Remove to a plate.

2. Beat eggs and cream in a bowl.

3. Melt remaining butter in the skillet and add mixture from bowl.

4. Add salt and pepper, to flavor, and stir constantly, until almost set.

5. Add lox and onions, stirring until heated throughout.

6. Spread on toasted bagel halves.

Silky Onion Soup

Description

Enjoy this tasty soup with a few carrot sticks and a piece of Melba toast. The creamy rich flavor will remind you of an elegant evening meal, instead of a lunch time treat.

Yields: 8 Servings

Ingredients

3 Tablespoons butter
1 sliced onion
2 garlic cloves, minced
2 leeks (white part only), cut in 1/2" strips
1 medium zucchini, sliced
½ teaspoon tarragon
¼ teaspoon salt
¼ teaspoon pepper
2 cups scallions, thinly sliced
28 ounces chicken broth
1 ½ cup water
½ cup heavy cream

Instructions

1. Melt 2 Tablespoons butter in a saucepan, over medium heat.

2. Add onion, garlic, leeks, zucchini, tarragon, salt and pepper.

3. Cover and simmer about 7 minutes
4. Stir in 1 ¾ cup scallions and cook until wilted.

5. Add broth and water and increase the heat until all is boiling.

6. Reduce heat and simmer for 10 minutes.

7. Remove from heat and break up the vegetables with a masher.

8. Return to a medium heat and add the remaining butter and the cream.

9. Heat just until boiling begins.

10.Remove from heat and sprinkle with remaining scallions.

Makes a great make ahead meal for warming up when on the run.

Tuna Salad Supreme in Tortilla Shells

Description

Give new meaning to tired tuna salad that grows old after a time or two. The right mix of veggies and a complementary bowl will turn tuna into a sought after lunch.

Yields: 4 Servings

Ingredients

4 8-inch round flour tortillas
1 Tablespoon olive oil
3 5-ounce cans Albacore tuna, drained
6 stalks celery, chopped
1 cucumber, peeled and cubed
2/3 cup mayonnaise
16 cherry tomatoes, quartered
4 lettuce leaves

Instructions

1. Heat oven to 400-degrees.

2. Take 4 oven-proof bowls and turn upside down.

3. Brush both sides of the tortillas with olive oil and place one over each bowl.

4. Bake in the oven until the tortillas are crisp and hold their shape, about 7 to 10 minutes.

5. Remove from oven and keep draped over the bowls until completely cooled.

6. In a bowl, mix the remaining ingredients (except the lettuce leaves).

7. Invert the bowls and lace each one with a lettuce leaf before adding the tuna salad.

You will never eat tuna salad on bread again!

Low-Cal Greek Salad

Description

Never miss out on the taste of feta cheese, blended perfectly in a luscious bed of romaine lettuce. Here is a great way to give in to your taste bud desires, without adding unwanted carbohydrates.

Yields: 1 Serving

Ingredients

8 leaves romaine lettuce, torn
1 cucumber, peeled and sliced
1 chopped tomato
½ cup red onion, sliced
½ cup low-fat feta cheese, crumbled
2 Tablespoons olive oil
2 Tablespoons fresh lemon juice
1 teaspoon dried oregano leaves
½ teaspoon salt

Instructions

1. Mix torn lettuce, cucumber, tomato, onion, and cheese in a large serving bowl.

2. Using a separate bowl, whisk together the oil, lemon juice, oregano, and salt.

3. Pour over salad.

Spinach Salad with Chicken and Raspberry

Description

Raspberry adds a tangy flavor to salads and chicken, so why not combine them? Adding a few other tricks will make this mid-day meal something to look forward to.

Yields: 4 Servings

Ingredients

¼ cup white vinegar
5 Tablespoons olive oil
1 teaspoon honey
½ teaspoon orange peel, shredded
½ teaspoon salt
¼ teaspoon pepper
4 skinless, boneless chicken breast halves
5 cups torn spinach
5 cups torn mixed greens
1 cup fresh raspberries
1 papaya, peeled, seeded and cubed

Instructions

1. Combine the vinegar, 4 Tablespoons olive oil, honey,

orange peel, salt and pepper.

2. Pour into an airtight jar and shake well. Store in the refrigerator to chill.

3. In a large skillet, heat over medium heat and add the remaining oil .

4. Add the chicken breasts and cook for 10 to 15 minutes, turning often, to brown all sides.

5. When no longer pink, remove from the skillet and pat out any excess oil and water.

6. Cut the warm chicken into thin strips.

7. In a large bowl, toss the greens, spinach and chicken strips.

8. Take your salad dressing and pour over the salad, tossing well.

9. Add the raspberries and cubed papaya, tossing gently.

Lettuce Roll-Ups with Pumpkin Seed Pate

Description

Move over hamburgers. This flavorful rendition of what used to be a sandwich, will make you wonder why anyone would choose meat over fresh veggies. Filled with marinated vegetables and seasoned with a unique pate, all your friends will want your recipe.

Yields: 6 Servings

Ingredients

6 large lettuce leaves

Marinated Vegetables:

2 stalks celery, sliced in 2-inch strips
1 cup carrots, shredded
¼ cup red onion, thinly sliced
2 Tablespoons flax oil
2 teaspoons lemon juice

Pate:

1 ½ garlic cloves

juice from 1 squeezed lemon
1 cup pumpkin seeds, soaked and sprouted
¼ cup flax oil
¾ teaspoon salt
¼ cup fresh parsley
¼ cup fresh basil
¼ cup dill
1/8 teaspoon turmeric
½ teaspoon fresh rosemary

Instructions for Pate

1. Using a food processor, place the garlic and pumpkins seeds inside and chop.

2. Add the lemon juice and mix until creamy.

3. Add the herbs and seasonings.

4. Pulse to finely chop all the herbs.

5. Spoon into a bowl.

Instructions for Assembly

1. Place all ingredients for marinated vegetables in a medium bowl and coat all pieces.

2. Lay flat a lettuce leaf and spread on a generous amount of pate.

3. Add ½ cup of marinated vegetables.

4. Roll up, folding the top and bottom to secure.

Chapter 3: Great Dinner Surprises

Mushroom Laced Meatballs

Description

You don't have to tell the family that they are on a low calorie diet when serving up dishes that are guaranteed to hit the spot. Lean hamburger will be anything, but boring, when dressed up with the right spices. See if anyone believes you when you admit that this dish has only 300 calories per serving.

Yields: 6 Servings

Ingredients

1 pound ground beef
1 egg
1/2 cup whole wheat bread crumbs
4 ounces shredded cheddar cheese
1/4 cup onion, chopped
1 Tablespoon Worcestershire sauce
1 Tablespoon fresh parsley, chopped

1/2 teaspoon basil
1/2 teaspoon pepper
1 Tablespoon oil
1 cup sliced mushrooms
1/2 cup beef broth
1/2 cup cooking wine

Instructions

1. Mix together meat, egg, bread crumbs, cheese, onion, Worcestershire sauce, parsley, basil and pepper.

2. Shape into 12 meatballs.

3. Add oil to skillet and brown meatballs on all sides, about 5 minutes.

4. Remove meatballs and dry on paper towels.

5. Add mushrooms to the drippings in the skillet and cook over medium heat for 2 to 3 minutes.

6. In a small bowl, mix flour, broth and wine until blended.

7. Pour over mushrooms and cook until boiling, stirring constantly.

8. Turn down heat and simmer sauce for 2 minutes.

9. Add meatballs to the creamy mixture and warm thoroughly, before serving.

Sassy Cheese and Chicken Enchiladas

Description

Kids will come running when they smell the succulent aroma of one of their favorite meals. Chicken enchiladas always top the favorites list, especially when dripping with cheese sauce. Microwave the entire meal and save time.

Yields: 6 Servings

Ingredients

2 cups cooked chicken breasts, chopped
1/2 cup chopped onion
1 garlic clove, minced
1 Tablespoon oil
4 ounces chopped green chilies
1/2 cup chicken broth
2 teaspoons chili powder
1 teaspoon cumin
4 ounces cubed cream cheese
6 6-inch flour tortillas
1/4 pound Colby or Cheddar cheese, cubed
2 Tablespoons milk
1/2 cup fresh chopped tomato

Instructions

1. In a 2-quart microwavable dish, mix onion, garlic and oil.

2. Microwave on high for 2 minutes. Stir and return for 1 more minute.

3. Remove and add chicken, chilies, broth and seasonings. Blend well.

4. Return to microwave and cook on high for 4 minutes.

5. Remove and add cream cheese, stirring until all the cheese is melted.

6. Spoon 1/2 cup of the mixture onto a tortilla shell and roll up. Repeat 6 times and place all, seam side down, on a flat microwavable dish.

7. In a clean microwavable dish, mix the Colby or Cheddar cheese, milk and 1/4 cup tomato and microwave on high for 1 minute. Stir and return for another 1 or 2 minutes.

8. Remove the cheese sauce and pour over the

enchiladas.

9. Microwave on high for 4 minutes.

10.Remove and top with remaining tomatoes.

11. Return to the microwave and cook on high for another 2 to 3 minutes.

Serve with salsa and chips.

Colorful Veggie Meatloaf

Description

Put sparkle in an old dish by using creative, and healthy vegetables. This one dish meal will add new meaning to meatloaf, as it was once known.

Yields: 8 Servings

Ingredients

1 1/2 pounds lean ground beef
3 cups white bread crumbs, toasted
1 cup diced tomatoes
1 cup fresh or frozen green beans (thawed)
1 egg
1 carrot
2 Tablespoons Worcestershire sauce
1 1/2 teaspoons salt
1/4 teaspoon pepper
1/4 cup ketchup

Instructions

1. Preheat oven to 375 degrees F
2. In a large bowl, mix all ingredients (except ketchup),

until well blended.

3. Turn into a loaf pan and top with ketchup.

4. Bake for 50 to 60 minutes, or until cooked throughout.

5. Remove and transfer to a platter, patting dry any excess fat.

Serve with a tossed salad for a filling, low calorie dinner.

Grilled Summer Kabobs

Description

Grilling during the spring and summer months can be exciting. The smell of meat that is char-broiled to perfection, can get your tummy growling. Make a delightful and low carb dinner, while including steak. A little bit goes a long way with this recipe.

Yields: 6 Servings

Ingredients

1 1/2 pounds boneless beef sirloin steak, cut into strips
1 zucchini, cut in 1-inch pieces
1 squash, cut into diagonal pieces
2 onions, quartered
12 cherry tomatoes
1/2 cup mayonnaise
1/2 cup plain yogurt
1/4 cup lemon juice
3 cloves garlic, minced
2 teaspoons minced ginger root
1/2 teaspoon cardamom
1/2 teaspoon cumin
1/2 teaspoon coriander

1/8 teaspoon red pepper

Instructions

1. Prepare the marinade by blending all seasonings, mayonnaise, yogurt and lemon juice. Put 1/2 cup of dressing aside for later.

2. Skewer the steak strips between the zucchini, squash, onions, and tomatoes.

3. Place the kabobs on a hot grill and brush with the marinade.

4. Grill for 10 or 15 minutes, or until the meat reaches the required doneness, turning and brushing twice.

5. Remove and serve with the reserved dressing.

Veggie Laced Macaroni and Cheese

Description

Macaroni and Cheese, from a box, offers little in the way of low carbs and vitamins. However, it will not take long for family to miss this simple mix of cheese and pasta. Try this homemade version that has a new twist and watch them ask for more.

Yields: 4 Servings

Ingredients

9 ounces penne noodles
1 ½ cups sharp cheddar cheese
1 Tablespoon tarragon
1/8 teaspoon ground white pepper
4 carrots, peeled and sliced
juice from one fresh orange
¼ cup water

Instructions

Warm oven to 350 degrees F.

In a saucepan, combine the carrots and juice from

orange.

Add l/4 cup water and heat until boiling.

Turn down, cover and simmer for about 30 minutes.

Remove from heat and transfer to a blender.

Puree contents.

In a separate pan, boil the penne noodles in salted water until al dente.

Drain off the water, reserving 1 cup in the pan.

Add the drained pasta to the pan, along with the puree.

Heat on medium, stirring to coat penne.

Cook, stirring often,
Add 1 cup cheese, tarragon and white pepper.

Once the mixture becomes creamy, pour all into a greased baking dish.

Add the remaining cheese on top and bake for 20 minutes.

Remove and let stand for 5 minutes before serving.

Chapter 4: Unique Side Dishes

Fake Mashed Potatoes

Description

If your family craves meat and potatoes, this is just an old habit. However, you can give them what they want by serving a meat dish and using this unique recipe for mashed potatoes, made from fresh cauliflower. The flavor will be better, the consistency, fluffy, and that mindset of meat and potatoes will quickly dissipate.

Yields: 4 Servings

Ingredients

1 fresh cauliflower head
1 Tablespoon water
1 Tablespoon butter
2 Tablespoons heavy cream

Instructions

Chop cauliflower into small pieces and add to a large

casserole dish.

Add 1 Tablespoon water, cover, and microwave on high for 5 minutes.

Remove and let stand for 5 minute.

Drain water from cauliflower and place in a food processor.

Add butter and heavy cream.

Process until smooth.

Scoop out and place in a serving bowl.

Simplistic Green Beans

Description

Sometimes the best things in life are amazingly simple. Take this green bean dish, for example. Only two ingredients deliver taste and fulfillment, complimenting any main dish.

Yields: 4 Servings

Ingredients

1 pound fresh green beans
1 onion, cut in half and sliced thick
1 Tablespoon oil
2 Tablespoons butter
Unrefined sea salt and pepper to taste

Instructions

Using a heavy skillet, sauté green beans, over medium heat, in oil and 1 Tablespoon of butter.

Add onion pieces and continue sautéing until the onions brown.

Turn into a serving bowl and let guests season, to their liking, with salt and pepper.

Dressy Cauliflower Casserole

Description

Cauliflower is a great food for keeping carbs low, but can become quite boring when prepared over and over again. This recipe dresses up this vegetable by using other seasonings for a flavor that almost makes you forget about the main ingredient.

Yields: 6 Servings

Ingredients

1 fresh head cauliflower, broken up, or 1 16 ounce frozen bag, cooked and drained
½ cup onion, diced
1 ½ cup fresh mushrooms
2 Tablespoons butter
¼ cup heavy cream
¼ cup mayonnaise
4 ounces shredded cheddar cheese
¼ cup green onions, chopped

Instructions

Warm oven to 350 degrees F.

Place prepared cauliflower in a greased 2-quart casserole dish.

In a skillet, sauté onion and mushrooms in the butter.

Add to the cauliflower and mix.

Mix in cheese.

In a small bowl, combine cream and mayonnaise.

Pour the sauce over the cauliflower mix and coat well.

Sprinkle the top with green onions.

Bake, covered, for 25 minutes.

Remove lid and bake another 10 minutes, or until the top is brown and crispy.

Chapter 5: Fulfillment with Drinks

Pina Colada Smoothie

Description

Soft drinks and some fruit drinks can be loaded with sugar. By side-stepping this calorie boosting substance, drinks take on a more lasting flavor, keep you from tiring and give your body the liquids that they need.

Yields: 2 Servings

Ingredients

1/2 cup unsweetened coconut milk
1/4 cup plain yogurt
1/2 cup fresh pineapple chunks
1/4 teaspoon coconut extract
1 teaspoon fresh lime juice
8 ice cubes
2 packets sugar substitute
2 lime slices

Instructions

1. In a blender, add all ingredients (except lime slices).

2. Blend on high until smooth.

Add a slice of lime to the edge of each glass to add a zesty twist.

Refreshing Fruit Shake

Description

Shakes do not have to weigh you down with unhealthy calories and leaving you feel sluggish. Try this homemade version of a strawberry milkshake and forget the tired feeling. Double the recipe to share with a friend.

Yields: 1 Serving

Ingredients

1 cup strawberries
1 cup almond flavored low-fat milk
1 packet sugar substitute
1 cube tofu
1 cup ice cubes

Instructions

1. Blend together strawberries, milk, sugar substitute, and tofu in a blender.

2. Add ice cubes and blend again.

Awesome Juice Spritzer

Description

Keeping the kids (and adults) away from soft drinks can be a never ending chore. Keep a 2-liter bottle of refreshing juice spritzer in the frig and no one will even miss the pop.

Yields: 6 Servings

Ingredients

9 ounces pineapple, orange, or pomegranate juice
48 ounces club soda or sparkling water

Instructions

1. Add juice to club soda or sparkling water, using a 2 liter air tight bottle.

Freshly processed and strained fruit can also be used in the place of juice.

Honey Dew Smoothie

Description

Add variety to your beverages by using a little thought of ingredient. The flavor will bring a new twist to boring fruit juices. Light and healthy, this drink only has 110 calories per serving. Increase ingredients to share with family and friends.

Yields: 2 Servings

Ingredients

4 cups cubed honey dew
2 apples, peeled, cored and cubed
2 kiwi fruits, peeled and sliced
3 packets sugar substitute
2 Tablespoons lemon juice
2 cups ice cubes

Instructions

1. Combine all ingredients (except ice cubes) in a blender and blend well.

2. Add ice cubes and blend until ice becomes broken

into small pieces.

Apricot Peach Slush

Description

This fruity drink has become a favorite of diabetics because of the sweet flavor and smooth texture. It's hard to think that something so refreshing can be good for you, but it is. Keep plenty of apricot nectar on hand because this beverage will go fast.

Yields: 6 Servings

Ingredients

15 ½ ounces apricot nectar, chilled
2 fresh peaches, peeled, pitted and sliced
1 ½ cups crushed ice
1 Tablespoon lemon juice
1 ½ cups chilled carbonated water

Instructions

1. In a blender, combine the apricot nectar, peaches, lemon juice and crushed ice.

2. Blend until smooth.

3. Spoon into a tall glass, filling halfway.

4. Fill the glass to the top with carbonated water.

Smooth Strawberry Passion

Description

Forget the milkshakes and all the calories and instead, make up a batch of Smooth Strawberry Passion drinks. Low in carbs and fat, this drink is great for a gathering or just to sit on the porch on a hot summer day.

Yields: 6 Servings

Ingredients

4 cups fresh strawberries, sliced
1 banana
1 kiwi fruit
16 ounces vanilla yogurt
1 cup ice cubes

Instructions

Using a blender, add strawberries, banana, and yogurt.

Blend until creamy.

Add ice cubes, one at a time, blending until they are broken up.

Pour in glasses, garnishing with kiwi fruit.

Wean Off of Soft Drinks

In a world of perfection, you would cut out all soda. The sugary sweeteners, found in soda, is almost impossible to break down. However, the addiction to soft drinks can cause you to abandon a new eating plan, after a day or two. If you currently have sugary soda in your daily life, definitely change to a diet brand - but don't try to cut it out cold turkey. You want to succeed in your new diet, so it is okay to start out slow. Slowly wean yourself off of the addictive, artificial taste by trading for a more refreshing taste of natural ingredients.

Chapter 6: Make Ahead Snacks

Sweet Popcorn Extravaganza

Description

Showtime in front of the TV will become even more exciting when there is a big bowl of crunchy, sweet snacks ready for each turn. Make this light and wholesome finger food ahead of time and keep in an air tight container.

Yields: 8 Servings

Ingredients

4 Tablespoons butter, melted
2 egg whites
2 packets sugar substitute
½ teaspoon vanilla extract
½ teaspoon cinnamon
¼ teaspoon salt
1 ½ cups low-carb cereal flakes
3 ounces pecans or almonds
4 cups pop corn

Instructions

1. Heat oven to 300 degrees F.

2. Lay a sheet of aluminum foil over a baking sheet and spray with Canola oil.

3. In a small bowl, combine butter, egg whites, sugar substitute, vanilla, cinnamon and salt.

4. Whisk the egg mixture until well blended.

5. Using a large bowl, add cereal and nuts and coat with the melted butter.

6. Add popcorn and lightly toss.

7. Pour mixture onto the baking sheet and spread evenly.

8. Bake for 20 to 25 minutes, or until crispy.

9. Remove and cool.

Store in an air tight container until show time. By adding the popcorn to the mixture last, there will be less clumps for hands to grab.

Granola Mini Balls

Description

These little bundles are the perfect size for snacking or grabbing as a quick energy picker-upper. Leave a plateful on the table and the refrigerator door will have less activity.

Yields: 6 Servings

Ingredients

2 cups granola
½ cup raisins
½ cup pecans, chopped
½ cup dried apricots
1 cup low-fat dried milk
1 cup creamy peanut butter
1/3 cup honey

Instructions

1. In a large bowl, mix granola, raisins, pecans, apricots, dried milk, and honey.

2. Gradually add peanut butter, stirring until all

ingredients are well covered.

3. Using your hands, form into small balls and place on small squares of waxed paper.

4. Place the balls, including the waxed paper on a serving plate. The waxed paper will keep the balls from sticking to one another.

Homemade Sweet Granola Mix

Description

Teach your kids how to have a great snack by letting them help make this sweet, crunchy treat. They will learn how to eat healthier, plus have something to munch on while playing video games.

Yields: 8 Servings

Ingredients

1 cup rolled oats
1 cup almonds
1 cup unsalted peanuts
1 cup raw sunflower seeds
1 cup flax seeds
1 cup sweetened coconut flakes
1 cup dried cranberries
3 Tablespoons brown sugar syrup

Instructions

1. Preheat oven to 250 degrees F.

2. Line a baking sheet with parchment sheets.

3. Use a large mixing bowl and add all ingredients.

4. Mix well with a wooden spoon or spatula.

5. Spread onto the baking sheet and flatten.

6. Bake for 15 minutes.

7. Remove and break up the granola pieces.

8. Bake for an additional 15 minutes.

9. Remove and cool.

10. Place into an airtight container.

Healthy Workout Granola Mix

Description

Here is another type of granola treat that is favored by athletes after a good workout. However, it was soon found to be a favorite of youngsters, as well.

Yields: 8 servings

Ingredients

1 cup rolled oats
1 cup almonds
1 cup dried cranberries
1 ½ cups butter
½ cup brown sugar
2 Tablespoons honey
½ teaspoon vanilla extract

Instructions

1. Preheat oven to 375 degrees F.

2. Coat baking tray with spray canola oil
3. In a large bowl, combine the oats, almonds, dried cranberries, and ground cinnamon.

4. Blend well with a large wooden spoon or spatula.

5. Add the butter, brown sugar, honey and vanilla extract together in a separate bowl, blending well.

6. Pour the butter mixture into the dry ingredients and mix until all is coated.

7. Spread the mixture onto the greased baking tray and press down to flatten.

8. Place in the oven for 20 to 25 minutes.

9. Remove and cool.

10. Either cut into bars, or break up the pieces for a bite size treat.

Low-Carb Nachos and Fixings

Description

Many people admit that their toughest part of staying on a low-carb diet, is giving up chips. Here is a unique way to have it all. Chips, cheese, salsa, at an amazing 6.5 net carbs. The secret is in the chips and here is a way to have your cake and eat it, too.

Yields: 10 Servings

Ingredients

8 ounces low-carb soy chips
1 cup chopped black olives
4 ½ ounces chopped, mild green chilies
12 ounces cheddar cheese, grated
2/3 cup sour cream
2/3 cup salsa

Instructions

1. Move rack in oven to within 6 inches of the broiler and preheat to broil.

2. Line 2 baking sheets with aluminum foil and spray

lightly, with canola oil spray.

3. Arrange the soy chips on the baking sheets in a single layer.

4. Top each chip with olives and chilies.

5. Sprinkle with cheese.

6. Place in oven and broil for 45 to 60 seconds.

7. Remove and transfer to a platter.

8. Place sour cream in one small bowl and the salsa in another.

9. Serve together.

Crispy Fried Fish with Lemon Sauce

Description

Who says you can't have fried fish on a low-carb diet? Choose pollock, whiting, haddock or scrod, and don't forget the sauce.

Yields: 4 Servings

Ingredients

4 8-ounce fish fillets
1 egg
2 ounces baked potato chips, ground
2 Tablespoons water
2 Tablespoons canola oil
½ cup mayonnaise
3 Tablespoons fresh dill, chopped
2 teaspoons lemon zest, grated
¼ teaspoon pepper

Instructions

1. Spread chip crumbs on a flat surface lined with waxed paper.

2. In a wide bowl, whisk 1 egg with water and brush on each fillet.

3. Heat a non-stick skillet to medium heat and add 1 Tablespoon canola oil
4. Dredge each fillet through the crumbs and place in the hot skillet.

5. Turn each fillet once after cooking about 3 to 4 minutes, or until golden brown.

6. Gently remove to plates
7. In a small bowl, mix the mayonnaise, dill, zest and pepper for dip.

Chapter 7: Let's Have a Picnic

Oriental Cabbage Salad

Description

Summer comes with lots of potlucks and bar-b-ques. Trying to watch your eating habits can be very trying with hamburgers and hot dogs being served. Start bringing great side dishes to get togethers and introduce the crowd to great tasting foods.

Yields: 4 Servings

Ingredients

½ head grated, green cabbage
3 chopped scallions
2 Tablespoons sesame oil
2 Tablespoons rice wine vinegar
2 Tablespoons toasted sesame seeds

Instructions

1. In a large serving bowl, combine the cabbage,

scallions, oil and vinegar.

2. Toss well, then refrigerate.

3. Right before serving, add the sesame seeds and toss lightly.

Kickin' Deviled Eggs

Description

Deviled eggs are an all-time favorite at picnics, but these beauties will make the crowd stop and say, WOW! The special ingredient may surprise you, and certainly, anyone who indulges. With 1 gram of carbs and 178 calories, maybe it won't hurt to have a couple.

Yields: 20 eggs

Ingredients

10 large eggs
4 Tablespoons cream cheese
½ cup mayonnaise
2 Tablespoons fresh chives, minced
2 teaspoons wasabi paste
pepper
1 teaspoon sea salt

Instructions

1. Boil eggs in a single layer, using a large saucepan, for 7 minutes.

2. Turn off heat and cover saucepan for 15 minutes.

3. Drain water off and refill with cold water. Let stand for at least 10 minutes.

4. Peel eggs and cut in half, long way.

5. Remove yolks and place in a large bowl.

6. Add the cream cheese and wasabi paste.

7. Mash with a fork or masher until everything is blended and resembles small crumbs.

8. Stir in the mayonnaise and chives and add pepper to taste.

9. Place the yolk mixture in a pastry bag and squeeze filling into the white cups of the eggs.

10. Make a swirling motion, beginning with the outer layer and working to a point in the middle.

11. Just before serving, sprinkle with sea salt.

Chicken Waldorf Salad

Description

Everyone loves the flavor of apples and walnuts, mixed with greens and a tart dressing. Make it a meal by adding chicken and using a new kind of dressing that will make guests request, time and time again.

Yields: 4 Servings

Ingredients

4 cooked and cubed chicken breasts
1 cup chopped celery
1 ½ cup chopped apples
4 ounces walnut pieces
4 Tablespoons raisins
1 cup low-fat Italian dressing
10 cups Iceberg and Bibb lettuce

Instructions

1. Place the lettuce, chicken, apples and celery in a large serving bowl and toss well.

2. Pour the Italian dressing over all and toss to coat.

3. Add the walnut pieces and raisins, gently blending.

Fresh Green Bean and Tomato Italiano

Description

There is nothing more flavorful than the taste of fresh green beans that are served up steamed and crunchy. Bring this dish to your outdoor party and you will find that even the youngsters will be tempted with their presence. This is a quick and easy side dish that delivers a compliment to any type of meat.

Yields: 6 Servings

Ingredients

3 cups fresh green beans
2 plum tomatoes, sliced into thin wedges
2 Tablespoons fresh basil
¼ cup Italian dressing

Instructions

1. Steam green beans for 10 minutes, just long enough to remove the raw texture.

2. Cool and add tomatoes and basil.

3. Pour dressing over all and toss lightly, just to coat.

Confetti Pasta Salad

Description

Here is a dish that is almost too beautiful to eat. Colorful and robust, it will seem more like a main dish than a complimentary side. Increase the size to share for an outdoor BBQ or other picnic event.

Yields: 4 Servings

Ingredients

1 cup multicolored, low-carb penne, cooked
4 artichoke hearts, diced
4 ounces thinly sliced turkey breast strips
8 ounces fresh mozzarella, diced
4 Tablespoon red pepper
8 Tablespoons fresh, chopped green beans
4 Tablespoons olive oil
4 teaspoons balsamic vinegar
2 teaspoons fresh oregano, chopped

Instructions

1. Combine pasta, artichoke hearts, turkey, mozzarella, red pepper and green beans in a large salad bowl.

2. In a small bowl, mix oil, vinegar, and oregano.

3. Pour over the pasta mixture and toss.

Cobb Salad with Crab

Description

Seafood is the main ingredient that gives this salad a wonderful flavor. Along with other cobb salad favorite additions, this side dish goes very well with those lake-caught fish.

Yields: 4 Servings

Ingredients

12 cups romaine lettuce, torn into bite-size pieces
12 ounce cooked crab meat
2 cups cherry tomatoes, halved
1 cup crumbled blue cheese
½ cup olive oil raspberry flavored dressing

Instructions

1. In a large serving bowl, add lettuce, crab meat, tomatoes and blue cheese.

2. Toss well then add dressing and toss again.

Chapter 8: Exciting Desserts

Chocolate Sponge Cake with Strawberries

Description

There is something wrong with a low-carb diet that does not allow for the sweet pleasures in life, mainly cake and chocolate. This dessert will satisfy both with rich flavor and texture.

Yields: 10 Servings

Ingredients

7 egg whites
1/8 tsp cream of tartar
¾ cup sugar
3 egg yolks
1 teaspoon vanilla
1 cup cake flour
3 Tablespoons melted butter
1 ½ ounces semisweet chocolate
2 Tablespoons canola oil
12 plump strawberries

Instructions

1. Heat oven to 350 degr F.

2. Use a large bowl to beat the egg whites and cream of tartar until foamy.

3. Add the sugar, gradually, while whipping into a meringue, with soft peaks.

4. In another bowl, beat together the egg yolks and vanilla.

5. Add the egg yolk mixture to the egg whites, gradually, folding until well blended.

6. Fold in the flour, stirring until all has been absorbed.

7. Pour batter into the cake batter and fold gently.

9. Spoon the batter into a 10-inch tube pan and bake for 35-40 minutes, or until the center proves clean, with a tooth pick.

10. Remove the cake and turn upside down on a large bottle so all sides are exposed to the air.

11. Cool for about an hour.

12. Remove the pan and run a knife along the sides of the pan to loosen the cake, then invert onto a wire rack to further cool.

13. Place on a serving dish.

14. Melt the chocolate and oil, slowly to keep from scorching and drizzle over the cooled cake.

15. Dot the top with strawberries.

Luscious Lime Cheesecake Tarts

Description

Cheesecake can add the final touch to a great meal, or be a special treat for friends that visit. Adding the tartness of lime and the sweetness of kiwi, will let you savor every bite.

Yields: 12 Servings

Ingredients

12 vanilla wafers
¾ cup cottage cheese
8 ounces low-fat cream cheese
¼ cup sugar or sugar substitute
2 eggs
1 Tablespoon grated lime rind
1 Tablespoon fresh lime juice
1 teaspoon vanilla
¼ cup vanilla flavored yogurt
2 kiwis, peeled, sliced and halved

Instructions

1. Using a 12-cup muffin pan, line each cup with a paper

muffin liner.

2. Heat oven to 350 degrees F.

3. Place a vanilla wafer in the bottom of each cup.

4. Using a blender, add the cottage cheese, cream cheese and sugar. Blend well.

5. Add the eggs, lime rind, lime juice and vanilla. Beat until smooth.

6. Spoon the mixture into the lined muffin cups and bake for 15-20 minutes, or until well set.

7. Remove from oven and chill completely.

8. Right before serving, spread the vanilla flavored yogurt on top and garnish with kiwi pieces.

Fruity Bread Pudding

Description

Bread pudding can become a sinful dish when laced with peaches and cream. Serve up this delightful dessert to family and friends. Have the recipe ready to share because everyone will want to know your secret ingredients.

Yields: 12 Servings

Ingredients

1 teaspoon butter, softened
6 slices low-carb bread, cubed
1 ½ cups fresh or frozen chopped peaches
4 eggs
1 cup heavy cream
½ cup sugar
¼ teaspoon nutmeg
1 ½ teaspoons vanilla
2 Tablespoons sliced almonds

Instructions

1. Warm oven to 350 F degrees.

2. Butter an 8-inch square baking dish

3. Add bread crumbs and peaches to dish and toss.

4. In a medium-sized bowl, add eggs, cream, sugar, nutmeg and vanilla, and whisk together.

5. Pour the egg mixture over the bread and peaches.

6. Let stand for 10 minutes to allow the bread to absorb the liquid mixture.

7. Sprinkle almonds on top of the dish.

8. Place the dish inside a 9x11 pan, filled with boiling water. The water should rise halfway up the sides of the 8-inch dish.

9. Bake for 45 to 50 minutes, or until a clean knife shows that it is done.

Almond Ricotta Pudding

Description

Take a break with a smooth, luscious pudding that is satisfying and only 8 carbs per serving. Quick to make, this recipe is designed for 1 serving but can be stretched to include the whole family.

Yields: 1 Serving

Ingredients

½ cup ricotta cheese
¼ teaspoon almond extract
1 packet sweetener
1 teaspoon slivered toasted almonds

Instructions

1. Mix the ricotta cheese, almond extract and sugar substitute.

2. Sprinkle with almonds.

Enjoy.

Heavenly Chocolate Sorbet

Description

Remember the fudge ice pops that you enjoyed as a child? Here is an adult version that will bring back memories, yet satisfy the grown up you. You will need an ice-cream maker for this recipe. This treat is not for kids, the more reason to sneak away and enjoy.

Yields: 4 Servings

Ingredients

2 cups ice cold water
1 teaspoon unflavored gelatin
1 ½ cups sugar-free chocolate syrup
1 cup low-fat milk
3 Tablespoons dark rum

Instructions

1. Add 2 Tablespoons ice water in a glass measuring cup.

2. Sprinkle with gelatin.

3. Microwave for 20 seconds to dissolve the gelatin.

3. In a medium-sized bowl, add ¾ cup syrup, the remaining ice water, milk and rum.

4. Stir until blended.

5. Add the remaining chocolate syrup into the mix and whisk.

6. Add the dissolved gelatin and stir.

7. Pour the mixture into an ice-cream maker and churn, according to instructions.

8. Remove and place in an airtight container and place in the freezer until ready to serve.

Non Traditional Squash Pie

Description

Pumpkin pie may be the tradition, but there's a new version in town. Serve up this wonderful dessert that offers much lower calories and carbs and start a new traditional during the holidays, or any time.

Yields: 8 Servings

Ingredients

3 cups cooked winter squash, mashed
¾ cup unsweetened coconut milk
¼ cup honey
3 eggs
2 teaspoons pumpkin pie spice
1 ½ teaspoons maple extract
1 ½ Tablespoons arrowroot powder
1 ¼ teaspoons unrefined sea salt, finely ground
½ teaspoon sugar

Instructions

1. Warm oven to 350 degr F.

2. Mix all ingredients with a mixer or in a food processor. If the consistency is too thick, add a little water, 1 teaspoon each, until no longer stiff.

3. Pour into a greased 10-inch pie pan and bake for 50 to 60 minutes, or until a knife comes out clean, when placed in the center.

4. Allow pie to cool then chill for another 30 minutes, to firm.

Chapter 9: Wise Wok Cooking

Shrimp Egg Rolls

Description

Reintroduce your wok to keep fat and sugar limited. It may take some time to prepare these awesome egg rolls, but the results are well worth the trouble.

Yields: 8 Servings

Ingredients

½ pounds raw shrimp, cleaned and deveined
1 teaspoon sherry
1 teaspoon salt
½ teaspoon cornstarch
3 Tablespoons canola oil
3 cups diced celery
½ teaspoon sugar
1 Tablespoon water
½ cup fresh bean sprouts
1 cup shredded lettuce
1 cup chopped water chestnuts

16 egg-roll wrappers

Instructions

1. In a small bowl, combine shrimp, sherry, salt and cornstarch.

2. Let the mixture marinate for 12 to minutes.

3. Heat 1 tablespoon oil in work.

4. Add shrimp mixture and stir-fry until shrimp is pink and firm.

5. Remove to a mixing bowl.

6. Add remaining oil to wok and add celery, stir-frying for 2 to 3 minutes.

7. Add sugar and water.

8. Cover and let steam for 1 minute.

9. Remove cover and stir-fry until all the liquid has evaporated.

10. Add to shrimp mixture.

11. Add remaining ingredients.

12. Blend well.

13. Prepare wrappers by laying out flat.

14. Fill each one with ¼ cup shrimp mixture.

15. Lift lower triangle of wrapper over filling and tuck the point under.

16. Leave the upper point of the wrapper flat.

17. Bring the 2 end flaps up and over the enclosed filling and press flaps down firmly.

18. Brush cold water over the exposed triangles and roll the filled portion until you have a neat package. The water will seal your ingredients protectively.

19. Repeat until you have 16 filled egg rolls.

20. Fill the wok with 3 inches of oil in the center.

21. Heat to 375 degrees F.

22. Using tongs, lower 4 eggs rolls into the oil and deep fry for 3 to 4 minutes, or until golden brown.

23. Drain on paper towels, blotting out all of the oil.

24. Repeat until all egg rolls have been cooked.

Serve with hot mustard, plum sauce or soy sauce. You can also store for later use by cooling and wrapping in plastic wrap, then placing in freezer bags to refrigerate or freeze.

Mandarin Cauliflower and Broccoli Medley

Description

Making your vegetables more interesting, will create a reason for your family to try any new variation. The aroma of this mixture, while stir-frying, will have everyone sitting at the table, ready to enjoy.

Yields: 4 Servings

Ingredients

2 Tablespoons canola oil
½ teaspoon salt
10 mushrooms, sliced lengthwise
1 small onion, minced
1 cup water
1 ½ cups bite-size cauliflower pieces
1 ½ cups bite-size broccoli pieces
½ cup water
2 teaspoons sugar
2 teaspoons cornstarch dissolved in 1 Tablespoon water

Instructions

1. Heat oil and salt in wok.

2. Add mushrooms and onion.

3. Stir-fry for 2 minutes or until tender.

4. Add water and bring to a boil.

5. Cover and steam for 5 minutes.

6. Uncover and add broccoli.

7. Cover and steam for an additional 10 minutes, stirring occasionally.

8. Uncover and add remaining water and sugar.

9. Bring to a simmer and add cornstarch mix.

10. Stir until sauce thickens and all vegetables are well coated.

Stir Fry Chicken and Peaches

Description

A delicate sauce make this stir fry chicken recipe a hit with the family. Low-cal and nutritious, peaches all extra flavor to a classic sweet and sour classic dish.

Yields: 6 to 8 Servings

Ingredients

1 3-pound chicken, cut into 8 pieces
1 teaspoon salt
½ teaspoon poultry seasoning
3 Tablespoons cornstarch
1 cup canola oil plus 1 Tablespoon oil
1 clove garlic, peeled and crushed
8 ounces frozen sliced, unsweetened peaches, thawed
1 Tablespoon sugar
2 Tablespoons lemon juice
½ cup chicken broth
2 teaspoons cornstarch dissolved in 1 Tablespoon water
10 ounces frozen snow peas
3 cups hot cooked rice

Instructions

1. Fill wok half full with water.

2. Place chicken pieces in a shallow baking dish and sprinkle with salt and poultry seasoning.

3. Place dish on a wire rack atop the wok and cover.

4. Cover chicken and turn wok on medium-high.

5. Steam the chicken for 45 minutes.

6. Remove and dry chicken pieces.

7. Rub cornstarch into each chicken piece.

8. Remove water from wok and wipe dry.

9. Add 1 cup canola oil into wok and heat to just under sizzling.

10. Fry chicken pieces in the hot oil, 2 or 3 pieces at a time until lightly browned.

11. Remove to a plate, lined with paper towels.

12. Pour oil out of wok and discard.

13. Add 1 Tablespoon oil to wok, add garlic, and stir-fry until brown.

14. Remove and discard garlic.

15. Add peaches and sugar, snow peas, stirring into the garlic liquid.

16. Stir in lemon juice.

17. Add chicken broth and heat to boiling.

18. Stir in dissolved cornstarch.

19. Add snow peas, stirring into the liquid.

20. Cover and steam for 30 seconds.

21. Add chicken pieces to wok and cover.

22. Steam for 30 seconds or until chicken is heated.

Serve over hot cooked rice.

Oriental Rice

Description

It seems that every time you have a Chinese-type of meal, there is tons of white rice left over. Put it to good use with this tasty oriental rice recipe. It will make a great side dish for a lunch or dinner menu
Yields: 4 to 6 Serving

Ingredients

1 Tablespoon oil
2 cups cold cooked rice
½ cup chopped water chestnuts
½ cup raisins
¼ cup soy sauce

Instructions

1. Heat oil in wok.

2. Add rice and cook, stirring until coated with oil.

3. Add water chestnuts and raisins.

4. Stir-fry until all is heated.

5. Add soy sauce and blend well.

6. Turn into a serving bowl.

Small portions of leftover meat can also be used for additional flavor.

Sweet and Sour Shrimp

Description

Who doesn't love the awesome flavor of sweet and sour sauce, mixed with shrimp and fresh vegetables. Here is a recipe that will amaze your taste buds and satisfy your hunger.

Yields: 4 Servings

Ingredients

1 carrot, peeled and diagonally sliced
1 green pepper, cut into 1-inch squares
2 cups canola oil
½ teaspoon salt
8 ounces breaded, frozen shrimp
1 clove garlic, peeled and flattened
1 cup unsweetened pineapple chunks, drained (save the juice)
¾ cup mixed sweet pickles, drained

Sauce Ingredients

1 ¼ cup unsweetened pineapple juice
¼ cup white wine vinegar

1 Tablespoon soy sauce
1/3 cup brown sugar
1/4 cup catsup
2 Tablespoons cornstarch

Instructions

Prepare the Sweet and Sour Sauce first.

1. In a small saucepan, combine 1 cup pineapple juice, vinegar, soy sauce, sugar and catsup.

2. Stir over medium heat until simmering.

3. Dissolve cornstarch in ¼ cup pineapple juice and add to pan.

4. Stir until smooth.

5. Remove from heat and set aside.

Stir-Fry Section

1. Place carrot slices in saucepan and cover with water.

2. Boil for 5 minutes

3. Add green pepper and boil for another 5 minutes.

4. Drain and set aside.

5. Add oil and salt to wok.

6. Heat to 375 degrees F.

7. Fry the frozen shrimp, a few at a time, until lightly browned.

8. Drain on paper towels.

9. Remove oil from wok and wipe clean with paper towels.

10. Discard oil.

11. Add 1 Tablespoon oil to wok.

12. Set to high heat.

13. Add garlic, rubbing against sides and bottom until lightly browned.

14. Remove and discard.

15. Add peppers and carrots.

16. Stir-fry for 30 seconds.

17. Add the sweet and sour sauce.

18. Next, add the pineapple chunks and pickles.

19. Stir-fry until hot.

20. Add cooked shrimp and cover all with sauce.

21. Spoon over hot cooked rice.

Pears Cardinal

Description

No one will find these pears boring with the succulent flavor of raspberries, surrounding them. Easy to make while you have your wok out, or use your stove top. Attractive, rich and melt-in-your mouth consistency, make this dessert a great finish to any meal.

Yields: 8 to 10 Servings

Ingredients

6 ripe pears
Red food coloring
20 ounces frozen raspberries, thawed (or fresh is even better)
2 Tablespoons sugar
2 teaspoons cornstarch, dissolved in 2 Tablespoons water
¼ cup kirsch liqueur, or raspberry flavored syrup

Instructions

1. Place a rack in wok that is filled with simmering water.

2. Stand up pears on the rack and cover.

3. Steam for 10 to 15 minutes.

4. Remove pears from rack.

5. Run under cold water to gently remove skin.

6. Rub each pear with a little red food coloring for a blushed appearance.

7. Refrigerate until chilled.

8. Blend raspberries in a blender.

9. Strain out seeds.

10. Place the raspberry puree in a saucepan and bring to a boil.

11. Stir in sugar and dissolved cornstarch.

12. Keep stirring until mixture thickens.

13. Remove from heat and add liqueur or flavored syrup.

14. Refrigerate until well chilled.

15. When ready to serve, place on pear in a serving dish and spoon the sauce over the top.

Chapter 10: List of Low-Carb Foods

Trying to keep all of the terms straight, like carbohydrates, calories, low-fat, and induction, can be difficult to understand. Not all low-carb foods are low-fat, or low in calories. Start with this list of foods that can keep anyone on the straight and narrow in beginning a low-carb diet. After a while, you will learn, just by tasting, how some foods dull your palate in enjoying the rich flavor of natural foods. One of these is sugar. It is a known fact that refined sugar decreases your ability to savor flavor. By ridding your diet of refined sugar, bleached white flour, margarine, and other processed, synthetic additives, you will begin to enjoy the wholesome flavor that low-carb natural foods have to offer.

- Cucumbers
- Broccoli
- Iceberg Lettuce
- Celery
- White Mushrooms
- Turnips
- Radishes
- Romaine Lettuce

- Asparagus
- Green Pepper
- Okra
- Cauliflower
- Cabbage
- Red Bell Pepper
- Spinach
- Beets
- Green Beans
- Carrots
- Kale
- Sugar Snap Peas
- Corn
- Onions
- Watermelon
- Strawberries
- Cantaloupe
- Avocado
- Blackberries
- Honeydew Melon
- Grapefruit
- Oranges
- Peaches
- Papaya
- Cranberries
- Plums
- Raspberries
- Pineapple
- Nectarine
- Blueberries

- Apples
- Pears
- Kiwi Fruit
- Cherries
- Tangerines
- Mango

If you feel that you just can't stay away from refined sugar, try these natural alternatives in cooking and see how quickly your habit begins to fade.

- Molasses
- Sorghum
- Real Maple Syrup
- Maple Sugar
- Sucanat or Rapadura
- Agave Syrup
- Coconut Sugar
- Honey

Bread is a real obstacle for many that have grown up on products made from white flour. If you are able to find bread products with any of the following main ingredients, you will be doing your body a favor.

- Corn
- Soybeans
- Oat Bran
- Barley

- Organic Sprouted Wheat
- Millet

Pasta has grown popular in making quick meals but the ingredients can be full of carbs. While many companies are slow to transform a popular-selling product into one that offers good nutrition, one company is gaining ground because of the low-carb content. Known as Shirataki, the starch is made from the root of devil's tongue, a type of yam. While you will probably never find this product in your local grocery store, keep your eyes open for new types of pasta alternatives in the foreign cuisine section.

Chapter 11: Tips for Prepping

People raised in countries, outside of the United States, are constantly amazed at how our grocery shopping is done. They are used to shopping for fresh produce and seafood on a daily basis, not weekly, as is practiced in the states. How can anything be fresh when it is allowed to set for a week?

To say that it is simple to eat healthier on a low carb diet, according to American standards, would be misleading. Manufacturers of ready-made food stuffs , count on the fact that there is too little time to spend on healthy eating. Popping a cardboard box into the microwave or opening a can, has replaced wholesome foods with convenience. Unfortunately, this way of thinking has led us to where we are today. Weight gain, inadequate vitamin supply, and slow metabolism, is the result of pumping your body with preservatives and sugars that prevent a healthy system. While time is on everyone's mind, there are some short cuts that you can take to prepare for low carb meals.

Freeze, Freeze, Freeze

In the summer, fresh vegetables are everywhere. But

when winter sets in, finding produce can make your search for fresh foods, a real chore. This year, snap up those great looking veggies and freeze so you will have plenty on hand during the winter months.

Not all vegetables freeze well. Those with a high water content can become mushy and less flavorful, like onions and cucumbers. But many other types can retain their shape, presence and vitamins, for meal prepping. Here are some examples of vegetables that can be frozen and ready to use:

- Asparagus
- Beans
- Broccoli
- Cauliflower
- Squash and Zucchini
- Eggplant
- Snow Peas

How to Properly Freeze:

It is not difficult to prepare vegetables for future use, but it does take a little bit of planning. Pick a day for putting up your family's favorite veggies and follow these simple instructions to make an ample supply.

Supplies needed:

- 3-quart Saucepan
- Wire Basket
- Jelly roll pan
- Waxed paper
- Freezer Bags
- Marking Pen

Instructions for Blanching

Select your veggies and prepare by cleaning, cutting and making meal ready.

Fill the saucepan half full of water and bring to a boil.

Put the prepared veggies into the wire basket and plunge into the boiling water for 3 minutes.

Remove and drain. Pat dry to remove any excess water.

Line the jelly roll pan with waxed paper and lay out your vegetables in single file.

Place the jelly roll pan in the freezer, just long enough for the food to freeze.

Remove and place in freezer bags, squeezing out as much excess water, as possible.

Mark and date each bag and return to the freezer.

By getting into the habit of preparing garden fresh vegetables for future use, you can rest assured that your family will receive no preservatives or additives from packaged foods.

10 Tips for Staying on a Low-Cal Plan

No one claims that it is easy to break bad habits, but if you look at where you are, and where you want to be, anything is possible. Remember when you thought that using a cell phone was the most impossible thing you had ever done? But now you probably wonder how you ever lived without it. Everyone dislikes change but when the future turns out for the better, you wonder how you ever thought differently. Try some of these tips and you will soon be forgetting about those bad eating habits.

1. Use coconut as a sweetener. Why is coconut downplayed so much? It is a wonderful, sweet and tasty type of low-carb accessory that can become irreplaceable. Use it in main dish recipes, savor the juice and discover that it is very addicting.

2. Who started the rumor that eggs were bad? Eggs are

a great source of protein and can be eaten alone or used in salads and meals. They are also very portable for a quick energy boost. Use to make sauces, to add texture to foods, or just as a snack in the middle of the day.

3. Never throw leftovers away. You just spent a lot of time on a low-cal meal for your family and believe it or not, you have some scraps to deal with. You already know how good they are for you so wrap them up and use on a salad for lunch tomorrow.

4. Herbs are better than salt. We all have the habit of salting everything that is set in front of us. Break this habit by keeping a variety of herbs close by. The selection will be interesting and fun, plus a lot better than salt, which does nothing but harm your body.

5. Rice is a great filler but not the best when it comes to nutrition. Try something different, like ground cauliflower. The taste will not be so ho-hum and you might just trick your brain into thinking that it is rice, but somehow, even better.

6. Make good use of your muffin pan. Part of the problem with staying on a low- carb diet menu, is thinking that you are going to starve. The portions seem so tiny and your mind just cannot grab hold of the fact

that you will ever be satisfied. Start using a muffin pan to fill with portions so you will get used to having enough. Start with something filling, like pudding or chicken salad. You will be surprised just how much a muffin cup can hold.

7. Salads can be the spice of life. How many other foods are so flexible to accept fruit, meat, and vegetables, without ruining the taste? In addition, dressings and sauces can be an endless supply of flavor. From cheeses to herbs, lemons and limes, you can transform a salad into any flavor you desire.

8. Think of a lettuce leaf as a piece of bread and the need to be fulfilled with a sandwich, will slowly fade away. Wraps are becoming popular with anything and everything. Meat, cheese, pickles, or a mixture of favorite foods. Iceberg lettuce has big meaty leaves for wrapping up tuna salad, eggs, chicken breast, and more.

9. Go on an adventure to an Asian store and look at the labels of pasta. You will probably see some words that are foreign to you, but more than likely, they represent roots and vegetables instead of chemical additives that you do recognize. Asians are not big on bread and grains that make them feel sluggish. Ask someone in the market about the ingredients, or write down the names

and search for yourself.

10. If sweets are your downfall, don't deprive yourself and make the craving worse. Enjoy some chocolate or puddings that can be found on a low carb diet food list. Make ahead to keep on hand for when that craving hits.

Deciding to go on a low-carb diet is not just a choice for losing weight, but changing the way that you look at food. Our society has become accustomed to eating anything that announces 'low-fat' or 'low-carb, that we have been brainwashed into accepting almost anything. Always shop for fresh, or frozen, and learn to enjoy the taste of food that has been replaced with high fat and glucose filled preservatives. Not only will you feel better, but your weight will automatically begin to burn off and give you more energy.

www.ingramcontent.com/pod-product-compliance
Ingram Content Group UK Ltd.
Pitfield, Milton Keynes, MK11 3LW, UK
UKHW020144250726
13967UKWH00002B/853

9 781633 830790